DESTINATION:

Tokyo

A PICTORIAL HISTORY OF DOOLITTLE'S TOKYO RAID
APRIL 18, 1942

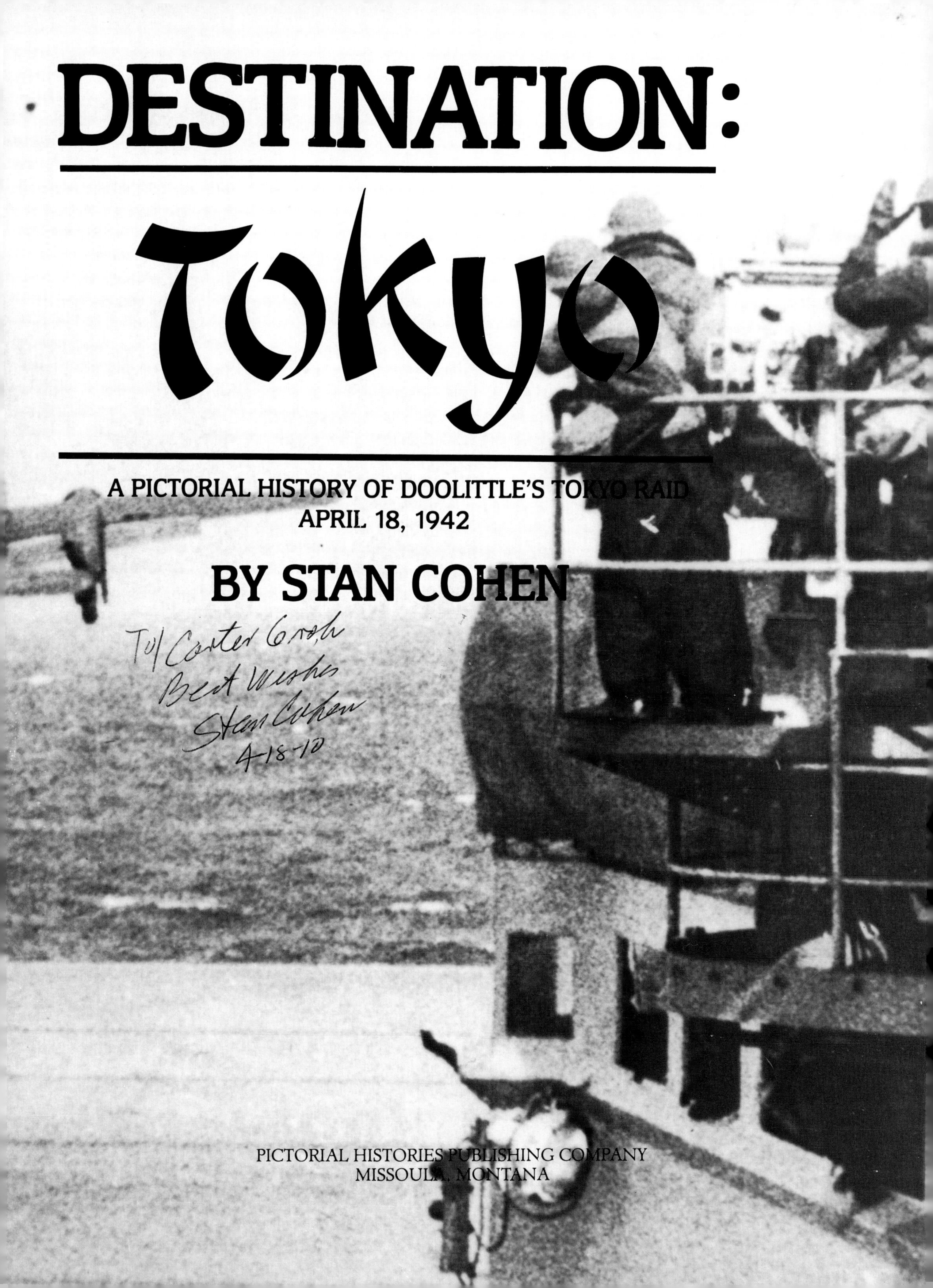

DESTINATION:
Tokyo

A PICTORIAL HISTORY OF DOOLITTLE'S TOKYO RAID
APRIL 18, 1942

BY STAN COHEN

*To Carter Grob,
Best Wishes
Stan Cohen
4-18-10*

PICTORIAL HISTORIES PUBLISHING COMPANY
MISSOULA, MONTANA

LIBRARY OF CONGRESS
CATALOG CARD NO. 83-60014

ISBN 978-0-929521-52-7

First Printing: April 1983
Second Printing: January 1984
Third Printing: January 1986
Fourth Printing: February 1987
Fifth Printing: September 1988
Sixth Printing: March 1992
Seventh Printing: March 1995
Eighth Printing: October 1998
Ninth Printing: March 2002
Tenth Printing: February 2004
Eleventh Printing: February 2007
Twelfth Printing: March 2010

BACK COVER EMBLEM

The gold shield denotes the excellence with which the Tokyo raid was accomplished. The B-25 ascendant in chief represents the leader, Lieutenant Colonel James H. Doolittle and signifies the successful takeoff and flight to target of all aircraft and crews. The men who flew the mission are represented by their squadron emblems on the quartered sphere, which alludes to a bomb sight and indicates the nature of the raid. The seven crosses chevronwise to honor point symbolize the outstanding overall support rendered the mission by the 17th Bombardment Group. The emblem bears the Air Corps colors, gold and ultramarine blue, and the national colors, red, white and blue.

Cover Art Work James Farmer, Glendora, California
Back Cover Courtesy General Richard Knobloch, San Antonio, Texas
Interior Art Work Joe Boddy, Missoula, Montana
Layout Stan Cohen

PRINTED IN CANADA

PICTORIAL HISTORIES PUBLISHING CO., INC.
713 South Third Street West, Missoula, Montana 59801
(406) 549-8488 fax (406) 728-9280
email: phpc@montana.com
website: pictorialhistoriespublishing.com

CONTENTS

MAPS

Destination Tokyo is an accurate and excellent pictorial and written description of the first aerial raid in Tokyo. It clearly depicts and presents the story of the raid.   —J.H. Doolittle

---

This book is dedicated to all 80 Tokyo raid participants.

PREFACE

Four decades ago 80 men volunteered for a top-secret, strategically and tactically important, and extremely hazardous undertaking. This was the first air raid on the islands of Japan on 18 April 1943.

Much has been written of that day 41 years ago when 80 brave Americans launched 16 B-25 aircraft from the carrier *USS Hornet*, but this is the first attempt to assemble in one publication a superb collection of photographs of this historic event.

This pictorial history explores the entire gamut of that event—from the Japanese aggressions in the early 1940s to present photographs of survivors. Many of these pictures have never been published before and were procured from government and private archives, as well as from the raiders themselves.

The men who participated in this mission were typical of those many dedicated Americans who have risked and sacrificed their lives for the freedoms of this great nation since its founding in 1776. Without volunteers such as the Doolittle Raiders this nation would long ago have disappeared in the annals of history.

May God bless those who are gone and those who remain.

—Stan Cohen, *April 1983*

INTRODUCTION

If World War II inflicted suffering and death on a larger scale than ever before, it also produced many acts of bravery and heroism that continue to stir our hearts. For sheer daring, danger and drama, Doolittle's raid must rank near the top of any such list. Though their short time over Tokyo scarcely scratched the paint on the Japanese war machine, the raiders achieved an important psychological victory. Few other events of the war had such an emotional impact on both the enemy and the American people.

I have tried to present pictorially the story of this remarkable raid, following the 80 American airmen through their training, the mission itself, and their adventures and misfortunes afterward. Though I have written a narrative designed to complement the photographs, this book is not intended to be a detailed historical study. For that, the reader is invited to consult Col. Carroll Glines' books, *Doolittle's Tokyo Raiders* and *Four Came Home*, which together constitute the best historical treatment of the raid. My volume should be regarded as a pictorial companion of the Glines books. For an excellent first-person account, Ted Lawson's *Thirty Seconds Over Tokyo* is recommended.

James Harper, staff writer for the *St. Petersburg Times*, covered the 40th reunion of the Tokyo Raiders in that Florida city in April 1982. His story brings the Raiders up to date and provides an appropriate introduction to this book:

Forty years after their deed was done, Jimmy Doolittle and his Tokyo Raiders met in St. Petersburg to look each other over, to call roll and to reminisce.

Why do old soldiers reunite? It is not, as some people assume, merely because they like to tell old war stories. Life has moved on—become too varied and precious for that.

They do it because, once, when they were very young men, they were required to do things they never thought they would have to do. Oh, in their boyhood dreams, they might have imagined being soldiers. But when the time came they found that war was more awesome, more frightening, more immediate in its bitter challenge, than they had dreamt.

Old Soldiers get together because once, when they were young, they faced death together—and survived.

How could a soldier forget these men?

⮞ Lt. Col. Jimmy Doolittle, whose confidence, skill and sense of duty helped him assemble a crack team of 80 fliers, navigators, bombardiers and gunners, then led them on a daring daylight raid from an aircraft carrier in the Pacific. It was the first time that such heavy-laden bombers had ever taken off a carrier. It surprised the Allies. It stunned the Japanese.

⮞ Cpl. Jacob DeShazer, who had a vision one day after 40 months as a Japanese prisoner of war. A voice told him, "Pray for peace, and pray without ceasing." DeShazer did not know that an American plane would drop an atomic bomb on Nagasaki that day. At 2 p.m. the voice told DeShazer, "You don't need to pray anymore. The victory is won." He returned to Japan in 1948 as a missionary. He worked there 30 years. One of his conversions was the Japanese officer who had led the air attack on Pearl Harbor.

⮞ Lt. Richard Joyce, whose plane shot down two others in dogfights over Tokyo. After the battle, he discovered a 7-inch hole in the rear fuselage, placed there by heavy anti-aircraft fire. "About all it did," he later shrugged, "was create quite a draft."

⮞ Sgt. David Thatcher, who alone escaped serious injury when his plane crashed near the coast of China. He helped his injured crewmates ashore and treated their wounds. He saved their lives and was awarded the Silver Star.

⮞ Lt. Horace "Sally" Crouch, who took note during his training about how different the health customs of China were from his native South Carolina. Instead of candy and cigarettes, he stuffed extra rolls of toilet paper into his flight bag as he left for the raid.

⮞ Tung-Sheng Liu, a Chinese engineer who spoke some English, who guided dozens of lost raiders through the Chinese countryside to safety in Chungking. Liu later moved to the United States.

⮞ Capt. Edward "Ski" York, who flew his plane from Japan to Vladivostock because it was burning too much gas to reach China. The landing was uneventful, but the Russians, who were neutral in the war with Japan, held York and his crew prisoner. They escaped 13 months later. "Communism, like a scab on the skin of the world, is spreading north, south, east and west," co-pilot Lt. Robert Emmens wrote later. "Fight it."

⮞ Lt. Robert Hite, who also survived 40 months of imprisonment by the Japanese. "I think," he said, "that even before I'd left Japan, I'd gotten over most of my hatred towards them." After watching his guards being beaten by their superiors he decided, "They were being pulled around by the ears just like we were."

These and 25 other men from the Tokyo raid were in St. Petersburg. Sixteen others are alive but could not come. Of the 80 original raiders, 31 are dead—some from the war, others from the passage of time. Three died in airplane crashes at the end of the raid; three more were executed by the Japanese; one died in prison of malnutrition. About a dozen widows joined the reunion in St. Petersburg.

At a solemn, private business meeting Saturday, the surviving raiders lifted their silver goblets in a toast [to their departed comrades].

There was also much merriment—although not quite a much as in 1947 when the group celebrated its second reunion in Miami Beach. The night watchman of the hotel reported to his manager that Doolittle and his boys ran around their halls in wet bathing suits until 5 a.m. "They were completely out of my control," he said. The manager later told Doolittle that the raiders had earned the right to make whatever noise they wanted.

Since then, the raiders have met 32 times in various cities around the country.

This time, the Edgewater Beach Motel on Tampa Bay was more sedate. There were fishing trips in the Gulf of Mexico, a fashion show for the wives, a golf tournament, a tour of the fighter planes at Mac-Dill Air Force Base.

They were joined for one day by Bob Hope, an old friend of the group. On Saturday, at a public banquet that ended the three-day reunion, they heard U.S. Sen. Barry Goldwater praise them for reviving American morale at the lowest point of the war. Goldwater also exhorted them to continue pulling for the country's strong defense. "You don't attack strength," he said. "You respect strength. A country that has strength is not going to war."

At a press conference, a television reporter tried to get Doolittle—now an 85-year-old retired lieutenant general—to comment on foreign policy and world affairs. Doolittle declined to pull rank on his commander-in-chief.

The same reporter asked Doolittle how he felt to be a major American hero. Doolittle simply replied, "I am pleased to be one of the Tokyo Raiders."

Acknowledgements & Photo Credits

Many people contributed to the production of this book. Generals Jimmy Doolittle and Richard Knobloch and Dave Thatcher provided help, encouragement and guidance. Many of the surviving raiders sent me photos and biographical information.

Archives were searched throughout the United States for photographs and information. Special thanks go to the staffs of the San Diego Aero-Space Museum, the Air Force Museum, the National Air and Space Museum, the Air Force and Navy Archives, the National Archives and the Academy of Motion Pictures Arts and Sciences. Also helpful were the Public Affairs offices of the Air Force Academy, Eglin Air Force Base and Rockwell International.

Individuals who helped included David Aiken of Irving, Tex., who supplied both information and Japanese photographs; Jeff Ethell of Front Royal, Va., and Jim Osbourne of Vincennes, Ind., who supplied photographs; and Mrs. John Fishburne of Tacoma, Wash., widow of Capt. C. Ross Greening, who allowed me to reproduce her late husband's paintings.

The cover artwork was produced by James Farmer of Glendora, Calif.; interior drawings are by Joe Boddy of Missoula, Montana. Bruce Donnelly did the maps, Mary Lou Hess the typing and Arrow Graphics of Missoula the typesetting. Charles Hood of the University of Montana School of Journalism edited the text and captions, and provided other editorial guidance.

Finally, my appreciation goes to my wife, Anne, and sons, John and Andy, who put up with countless inconveniences during the many months I worked on this book.

Photo acknowledgements include the following abbreviations:

AFM—Air Force Museum, Wright-Patterson Air Force Base, Ohio

AMPAS—Academy of Motion Picture Arts and Sciences, Beverly Hills, Calif.

Eglin AFB—Office of History, Armament Division, Eglin Air Force Base, Fla.

NASM—National Air and Space Museum, Smithsonian Institution, Washington, D.C.

USAF—U.S. Air Force Archives, Washington, D.C.

USN—U.S. Navy Archives, Washington, D.C.

Military situation in the Pacific area, early 1942. Most of these islands would fall to the Japanese by April 1942.

CHAPTER ONE
BACKGROUND
RISING SUN
OVER THE PACIFIC

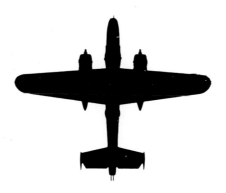

At the time of the Doolittle Raid—April 18, 1942—United States forces were in defensive positions throughout the world. American morale was not high. Much of the Pacific Fleet had been destroyed at Pearl Harbor four months before. Wake and Guam had been captured. The fall of the Philippine Islands was imminent, and would shrink the American defense perimeter to Midway and the Hawaiian Islands.

Japan had captured the Dutch East Indies,.Hong Kong and Malaya, and had sunk several British capital ships. The southern and western Pacific had become a Japanese lake.

The Japanese had launched their series of conquests in the early 1930s with the invasion of China. Milking anticolonist sentiment by advocating "Asia for the Asians," they had devoured massive quantities of land and resources during the next decade, all in the name of "The Greater East Asia Co-Prosperity Sphere."

Though Japan had signed the 1922 Washington Naval Treaty, which limited the size of the British, American and Japanese navies, it renounced the agreement in 1936 and built up its navy until it had reached parity with those of Great Britain and the United States.

In Europe, Germany and Italy were paralleling Japan's aggressiveness. Most of Europe and North Africa was under Axis domination. Germany was driving deep into Russia; some feared that Nazi and Japanese forces would link up in the Middle East.

Early 1942 was a desperate time for the Allied Nations. America needed a "shot in the arm," to restore its pride and to show itself and the rest of the world that it could carry the war to a formidable enemy. The Japanese had bombed American territory in a surprise attack at Pearl Harbor. What better response than to bomb the capital of Japan?

This photo was taken in April 1943 at an airfield at Kunming, China, headquarters of Gen. Claire Chennault's China Air Task Force (CATF). These flyers are all former Tokyo Raiders who were assigned to the 11th Bomber Squadron. Left to right: Sgt. Ed Horton, Sgt. Doug Radney (both on prop), Lt. Lucian Youngblood, Capt. Horace Crouch, Lt. Jacob Manch, Lt. William Fitzhugh, Capt. Clayton Campbell. Maj. Everett Holstrom, squadron commander, is in the cockpit.
Horace Crouch

CHAPTER TWO

CONCEPT THROUGH TRAINING

CAN IT BE DONE FROM A CARRIER?

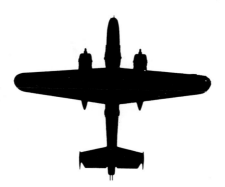

Since early January of 1942, President Roosevelt had advocated a bombing attack against the Japanese homeland to prick Japanese confidence and boost American morale, which had been hard hit by military disasters in the Pacific. It was assumed that the bombers would be land-based—in China, Russia or possibly the Aleutian Islands.

About this time Navy Capt. Francis S. Low, an operations officer on the staff of the Chief of Naval Operations, visited the naval base at Norfolk, Va., to check on the readiness of a new aircraft carrier, the *Hornet*. Flying over Norfolk, the officer noticed twin-engine bombers making simulated attacks on the outline of a carrier deck that had been painted onto a base runway.

That sight produced the idea for a mission that would stun the Japanese and delight the Allies scarcely three and one-half months later. Low returned to Washington with a novel proposal for his boss, Adm. Ernest King: Why not strike Japan using Army Air

Force bombers launched from the deck of a carrier? Certainly the Japanese would not expect such an attack—twin-engined aircraft, because of their size and weight and take-off distance needed, were considered impractical for carrier use.

Capt. Donald B. Duncan, King's air operations officer, took five days to develop the plan that—with some modification—would be carried out in mid April.

Before America's entry into the war, a famous American aviator, James H. Doolittle, had persuaded his old friend Gen. Henry "Hap" Arnold, Chief of the Army Air Force, to let him back into the Air Corps from which he had resigned in 1930. Doolittle, who saw war clouds gathering in Europe, was made a major on July 1, 1940, and was assigned to posts in Indianapolis and Detroit, where he helped convert the American auto industry to wartime production.

In January 1942, Doolittle was transferred to Arnold's staff, where he was placed in charge of the Air

Force's part in the mission to bomb Japan. Arnold could not have picked a more capable or enthusiastic officer for the job. Soon "Jimmy" was promoted to lieutenant colonel and was devoting all his time and energy to a project so secret that only a handful of people knew about it before the planes were launched from the *Hornet* in mid April.* The mission had no colorful code name—it was simply designated, "Special Aviation Project No. 1."

Doolittle's official report of the raid outlined the purpose of the mission:

The object of the project was to bomb the industrial centers of Japan. It was hoped that the damage done would be both material and psychological. Material damage was to be the destruction of specific targets with ensuing confusion and retardation of production. The psychological results, it was hoped, would be the recalling of combat equipment from other theaters for home defense, thus effecting relief in those theaters, the development of a fear complex in Japan, improved relationships with our Allies and a favorable reaction on the American people.

When the idea was conceived, there was no assurance that a heavy-laden bomber could take off from the short deck of a carrier, but on Feb. 1, 1942, off Norfolk, Lt. John E. Fitzgerald and Lt. James F. McCarthy each flew a stripped B-25 into the air from the flight deck of the *Hornet*.

Several bomber types were considered for the mission, including the B-18, B-23, B-25 and B-26. The B-18 was obsolete, with limited range and bomb load capacity; the B-23's wing span was too wide for a carrier deck; the new B-26, while having the necessary range and bomb capacity, was untried and—it was felt—too tricky to fly off a carrier deck. The B-25 seemed to be the best choice.

The original plan had the bombers returning to the carrier, but that notion proved to be impractical. The B-25's landing speed was too fast, and there were tailhook problems. It was decided to launch the bombers close enough to Japan to allow the pilots to fly on to safety in nearby countries. Vladivostok was only 600 miles from Tokyo, but the Russian government, which was not at war with Japan, refused American requests for an airmen's haven. That left Gen. Claire Chennault's Chinese bases, which were more than 1,200 miles from Tokyo. The crews that made it to those rough-hewn airfields were to be absorbed into the newly formed 10th Air Force and were to operate from that country against Japan. If the bombers were to have any chance of reaching the Chinese bases, they would have to be launched about 400 miles off the Japanese coast.

Planes and experienced airmen were not plentiful so soon after America's unexpected entry into the war, but the 17th Bombardment Group stationed at Pendleton Field, Oregon, had both the B-25s that the operation required, and the crews to fly them. This group, commanded by Lt. Col. W.C. Mills, was composed of the 34th, 37th and 95th Bombardment Squadrons and the 89th Reconnaissance Squadron, commanded by Maj. John A. Hilger. The aircrews were asked to volunteer for a dangerous mission that would be valuable to the war effort. More men volunteered than were needed. Twenty-four crews were selected.

Doolittle now had much to do and very little time to do it. The crews had to be selected and thoroughly trained in short take-offs and low-level bombing runs. The bombers had to be modified to provide a larger fuel capacity and better navigational aids. Special bombs had to be designed and targets selected in Japan. A Navy task force had to be assembled to escort the *Hornet* to within striking distance. The Chinese airfields had to be prepared to receive the planes, and to refuel them. And all this had to be accomplished with the utmost secrecy.

---

*Adm. King, Gen. Arnold, Capt. Low and Capt. Duncan knew of the project initially. Even President Roosevelt was not told all the details until April.

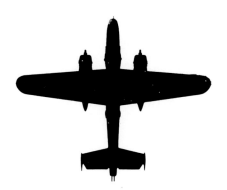

Other bombers were considered for the mission, but for various reasons were rejected. The pre-war Douglas B-18 (top) was too old, too slow and too limited in range. The Douglas B-23 Dragon (center) was a better aircraft, but its wing span was too wide for carrier operations. The new Martin B-26 Marauder (bottom) still had technical problems and required too much take-off distance.
USAF

Jimmy Doolittle early in his flying career.   AFM

After the raid Doolittle shakes hands with J.H. Kindelberger, president of North American Aviation, builder of the B-25 bomber. NASM (#A47141-E)

Lt. Gen. James Doolittle.

Lieutenant General James Harold Doolittle

The commander of America's first raid on the Japanese homeland in World War II was already a noted aviator when he was called on to plan that dangerous mission.

Doolittle was born on Dec. 14, 1896, in Alameda, Calif., but spent part of his youth and had his first taste of adventure in the gold mining camp of Nome, Alaska.

Graduating from Los Angeles Manual Arts High School in 1914, he attended Los Angeles Junior College and the University of California. He enlisted in the Signal Corps Reserve in October 1917, enrolled in the University of California's School of Military Aeronautics as a flying cadet, and got his commission in March 1918. During World War I he remained in the United States, teaching aerial gunnery and combat tactics for the Army Air Corps.

In the years after the war, Doolittle remained in the military, and gained national prominence as an aviator. On Sept. 4, 1922, he made the first transcontinental cross-country flight in fewer than 24 hours, flying from Pablo Beach, Fla., to San Diego in a DH-4 airplane.

He also continued his education. Taking advantage of his background in mining, he completed an A.B. degree in 1922 from the University of California, and an M.S. from the Massachusetts Institute of Technology in 1924. Just a year later he was awarded a Sc.D. from the same institution.

But it was Doolittle's skills as an airplane racer, not his advanced degrees, that continued to place him in the national spotlight. In the late 1920s and early '30s he won the "Big Three" of racing—the Schneider, Bendix and Thompson trophies. He took his place alongside the greats of early aviation.

Perhaps his greatest pre-war contributions to aviation were his experiments with "blind" all-weather flying. In a Consolidated NY-2 Navy Trainer, he made the first flight completely dependent upon instruments, on Sept. 24, 1929. The experiment proved that an airplane could fly safely in adverse weather or darkness and stimulated an aviation industry still in its infancy.

In 1930, Doolittle resigned from the Army Air Corps and was named manager of the aviation department of Shell Oil Co. in St. Louis. He helped develop better airplane fuels, which would prove to be of tremendous importance when the United States entered World War II. On temporary active duty with the Army Air Corps in 1932, he set a world speed record for land-based aircraft.

Doolittle was named president of the Institute of Aeronautical Science in 1940, but by this time he could see that war was imminent. He asked to be returned to active duty with the Air Corps. At the time of the Tokyo raid he was a lieutenant colonel; he was immediately promoted to brigadier general after its successful conclusion.

In September 1942 Gen. Doolittle assumed command of the Twelfth Air Force in North Africa and in March 1943 he was named commanding general of the Fifteenth Air Force in the Mediterranean Theater. From January 1944 to September 1945 he commanded the Eighth Air Froce in England and Okinawa. By war's end, his planes had bombed all three Axis capitals—Tokyo, Rome and Berlin.

Retiring from active duty after the war, he returned to Shell Oil as a director. Through the years he was associated with several other companies and served on numerous government boards and commissions.

His decorations included the Medal of Honor, the Distinguished Flying Cross with two Oak Leaf Clusters, the Bronze Star, the Air Medal with three Oak Leaf Clusters and numerous foreign honors. At present, Gen. Doolittle's medals and awards are on display at the National Air and Space Museum in Washington, D.C.

At the end of his career, Doolittle lived in Carmel, Calif., with his wife, the former Josephine Daniels, where he was a director of Mutual of Omaha Insurance Company.

He died in late 1993 at the age of 96. His wife, Josephine, preceded him in death.

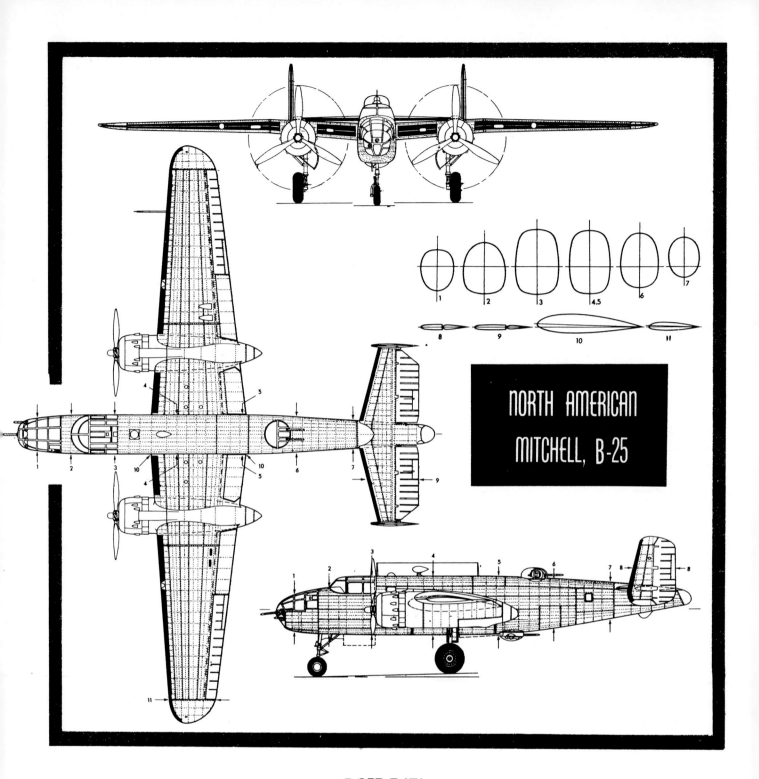

NORTH AMERICAN
MITCHELL, B-25

B-25B DATA

Number Built: 120 (one crashed before delivery)
AAF Serial Numbers: 40-2229-40-2242
40-2244-40-2348

Span: 67'7''
Wing Area: 610 Sq. Ft.
Length: 52' 11''
Height: 15' 9''
Max. Speed: 300 mph. @ 15,000'
Normal Bomb Load: 2,400 lbs.
Normal Range: 2,000 miles

Crew: 5
Empty Weight: 20,000 lbs.
Gross Weight: 26,208 lbs. (28,460 max. gross)
Power Plant: 2 1,700 hp 14 cylinder
Wright cyclone R-2600-9 engines
1,350 hp @ 13,000'

The B-25B

Of the several planes considered for use on the proposed Tokyo raid only the B-25B fit the requirements.

A twin-tailed, high-wing monoplane with a tricycle landing gear, the aircraft was designed in 1938 by North American Aviation of California in response to a government proposal for a twin-engined medium attack bomber. The plane was first designated the NA-40-1. A crew of five or six was needed to operate the plane, which was armed with .30-caliber machine-guns that were operated from a rotating nose blister, a dorsal power turret, two other locations in the fuselage and two fixed positions in the wings.

As that plane could reach a top speed of only 265 mph and carry no more than a 1,200 pound bomb load, it was not adopted by the Air Force.

Several design modifications were introduced prior to the awarding of a contract to North American on Sept. 20, 1939, for the construction of the plane designated NA-62. This was the bomber that eventually would be named the B-25 Mitchell, in honor of Gen. ''Billy'' Mitchell, an early advocate of air power.

The new version, flown for the first time on Aug. 19, 1940, was a distinct improvement over the earlier model. It reached a top speed of 322 mph and boasted a bomb capacity of 2,400 pounds.

When the United States entered World War II some B-25s were already in service. One had sunk a Japanese submarine off the West Coast.*

B-25s were used extensively by America and her allies throughout the war. They flew missions in every theater. There had been numerous modifications by the end of the war. One of the major improvements was the installation of a 75mm cannon in the nose on the B-25J Model, the heaviest weaponry ever installed on an American bomber to that time. The bomb capacity on later models was also greatly increased.

More than 9,800 B-25s were produced during the war. But only 119 of them were the B model—the Doolittle bomber.

*The plane was piloted by Lt. Everett W. Holstrom, one of the Tokyo Raiders. The submarine was sunk on Dec. 24, 1941.

A B-25B Mitchell Medium Bomber built by North American Aviation.

NASM

B-25B bombers at the Inglewood, Calif., factory in early 1942. USAF

Interior of a B-25B cockpit. USAF

B-25 Modification

The long range required of the bombers meant additional fuel tanks. A 225-gallon tank crowded the bomb bay area, and a 160-gallon receptacle occupied the crawlway above the bomb bay. The lower turret was removed to accommodate a 60-gallon tank, and the radio operator's compartment was stocked with 10 five-gallon fuel cans, whose contents were to be emptied into the rear tank before being punctured and dropped into the sea enroute. All told, each B-25 would carry 1,141 gallons. Even with the additional tanks, fuel would be a critical factor in the upcoming operation.

De-icers were installed in anticipation of receiving last-minute permission to fly to Russia. The secret Norden bombsight was replaced by a simple home-made aluminum sight. The Norden was considered too important to risk on such a dangerous mission, and, besides, the device was not useful at low levels.

Small electrically operated cameras were positioned

in the tails of six planes, including Doolittle's lead ship. On the other planes, 16-mm movie cameras were similarly mounted. None of the cameras were recovered.

Every expendable item was removed. Pyrotechnics were moved to less hazardous areas to reduce fire hazard. Most radio sets were left behind to reduce weight.

Each plane was to carry a mix of 500-pound demolition bombs with special fuses for low-level dropping and 500-pound incendiary bombs. All told, 30,000 pounds plus 7,500 pounds of demolition and 7,500 pounds of incendiaries were to be dropped on Japan by 16 planes.*

Many problems were encountered with the .50-caliber machine guns in the top turret and nose. The bottom turret was removed altogether because of problems with its operation and to make room for a 60-gallon fuel tank. Broomsticks were inserted in the Plexiglas tailcones, in hopes that enemy pilots would think they were machine-guns.

Most of the fuel tank modifications on the bombers took place at Mid-Continent Airlines in Minneapolis, Minn., before they were flown to Florida.

---

*The original plan was to take 18 planes on the mission. Sixteen planes were eventually loaded on the *Hornet*.

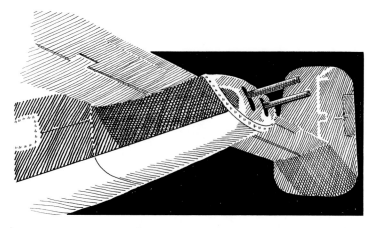

Broomsticks were put in the rear of the B-25s to simulate .50 cal. machine guns in hopes of warding off enemy planes.

The Mareng Cell

The Martin Aircraft Co. played an important part in the success of the Tokyo raid. Martin engineers developed a cell—the Mareng—to hold extra gasoline, so important to the extended flight the B-25s were required to make.

In January 1942, Col. Frank Cook, stationed at Wright Field, Ohio, made a hurried call to the Martin engineers. He requested that they design and supervise the manufacture of a flexible self-sealing fuel cell, to fit into a special cavity in the fuselage of a B-25.

Patent rights to a similar cell, capable of being made to fit any empty space desired, had been assigned to the company in 1937. This was the original Mareng Cell—a predecessor to the Mareng tank used during the war.

Col. Cook told the company that he wanted to store as much gasoline as possible in the crawlway of a B-25. He added that the project was both secret and urgent.

The engineers had only a few weeks to complete the job. Working from a meager set of B-25 blueprints, they designed a light synthetic rubber-coated container that, when full, would completely block the crawlway, whose structure would provide support for the fluid load. When empty, the cell could be rolled up and stored.

In Mishawaka, Ind., the U.S. Rubber Co. manufactured the cells and shipped them to Minneapolis, where one was installed in a B-25. Doolittle himself flew in to inspect the new tanks, and gave them his approval. The other B-25s, which were en route to Florida to train for the Tokyo mission, were ordered to stop at Minneapolis to be fitted with the Mareng cells.

Until the planes with their remarkable new fuel tanks were safely on board the *Hornet* two months later, military police guarded the planes constantly against spies. It was not until 1945 that the public was told of Martin Aviation's important contribution.

Mareng cells gave each B-25 an extra 160 gallons of gasoline, enough for 500 more miles of flying. The extra fuel tanks became even more important when it became necessary to launch the planes farther from the Japanese mainland than had been anticipated.

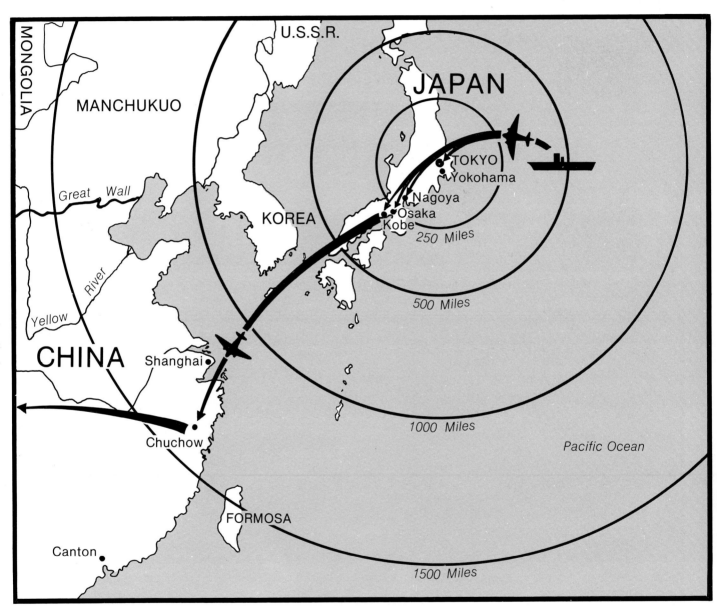

The initial plan for the raid: launch planes 400 miles from Japan, fly to airfields near Chuchow, China, refuel and fly to Chungking.

The Mark Twain Bombsight

This simple bombsight, used in all 16 of Doolittle's B-25s, was fabricated in the shops of Eglin Air Base in March 1942 using materials that cost 20 cents per device. It was developed by Lt. C. Ross Greening, pilot and armament officer of the group, to replace the top-secret Norden bombsight which cost over $10,000.

The bomb runs were to be made at 1,500 feet, a very low altitude for releasing 500-pound bombs. The Norden lost its effectiveness below 4,000 feet, and it was not designed for short bomb runs that might require violent maneuvers. It would be nearly impossible to sight targets through the Norden's optics as the bombers flashed over an unfamiliar city at low altitude.

Greening named his device the "Mark Twain" in reference to the simple "led line" depth finder used on the old Mississippi River steamboats. The sight was connected to the Norden linkages, thus permitting the bombardier to give aircraft turn directions to the pilot through the PDI (pilot direction indicator) instrument without relying on voice communications.

The dropping angle of the bomb was computed and the sighting bar set at that angle. The bombardier then had an open field of vision over the sight to direct the pilot to the target. When the target became aligned with the sighting bar, the bombs were released.

All of the original bombsights were lost on the raid. This one is an exact copy made by Lt. Col. Horace Crouch, USAF, Ret., navigator of Plane #10.

Training

Maj. John A. Hilger, commander of the 89th Reconnaissance Squadron, was designated as Doolittle's deputy. It would be Hilger's responsibility to train the 24 crews gleaned from the 17th Bombardment Group.

On Feb. 3, the 17th was reassigned to Columbia Air Base, S.C.; however, the airmen for the special mission were to continue on to Eglin Air Base in northern Florida, where their training would begin. Capt. Edward York and John Hilger were the only squadron commanders allowed to participate in the raid.

The aircrews and ground support personnel arrived at Eglin in late February and early March. None but Hilger knew anything about the special mission except that it would be dangerous and require intensive training.

Since part of the training was to be in short takeoffs, a veteran navy flier from the Pensacola Naval Air Station, Lt. Henry L. Miller, was assigned to the group. His assistance and knowledge were to prove invaluable in the months ahead.

Soon the roar of open-throttled B-25s was heard daily from an auxiliary field near Eglin. White lines simulating the limits of a carrier deck were drawn on two of the runways. Take-offs were practiced with a variety of loads, ranging from very light to overloads. The shortest take-offs were achieved by putting the flaps down full, the stabilizer at ¾ tail-heavy, increasing power against the brakes and then releasing the brakes when the engines reached the requisite rpms. A good headwind was required. The airplane left the ground almost in a stall situation, with the tail skid only a foot above the runway. After considerable practice, the aircrews managed to become proficient in light-load take-offs as short as 300 feet—good enough for a carrier launch.

Special training was also given in cross-country flying, night flying and navigation. Flights over the Gulf of Mexico gave pilots and navigators practice in operating without radio references or landmarks.

Low-altitude bombing practice, using both dummy and live bombs, was given a high priority. So was marksmanship by the gunners, who practiced machine-gun firing on the ground and in the air.

During this period, Doolittle was shuttling between Eglin and Washington, but he got in his own training time in the hope that he could lead the mission. Every aspect of the training was conducted in the strictest secrecy—word of the mission leaking out would have jeopardized the entire project.

By late March the training was complete, and time was getting short. If the target date of mid-April was to be met, the planes would have to be flown with their crews to California, and a naval task force formed to escort the raiders toward their destination.

Twenty-two of the 24 crews were ordered to report to McClellan Field at Sacramento, where additional work would be done on the planes. The other two crews were sent back to their home base in South Carolina.

From Sacramento, the B-25s were flown to the Alameda Naval Air Station near San Francisco, for loading on board the carrier *Hornet*.

The aircrews still did not know that their final destination would be Japan. But it was clear that they were going to bomb an important enemy target.

Checking stop watch times during short take-off practices at Eglin Field are, from left: Lts. Knobloch, McElroy, Joyce and Farrow. The pilots became proficient in these tricky take-offs, and all got off safely from the Hornet *on April 18.*   USAF

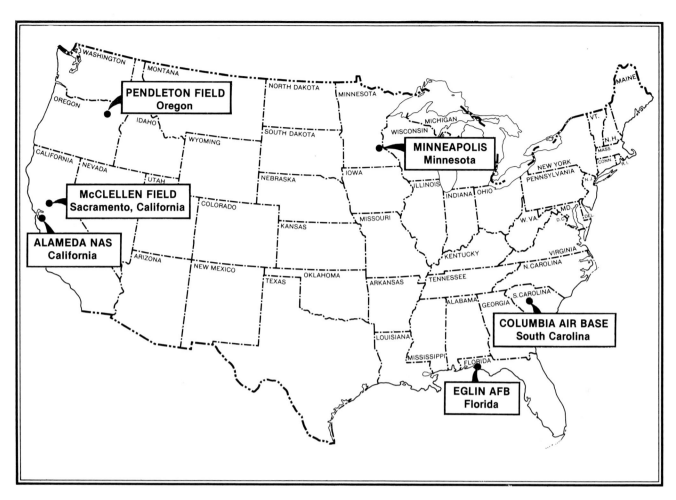

Tokyo Raiders training and repair sites, Jan.-April 1942.

The main entrance to Eglin Field in 1939. This is the present East Gate of Eglin Air Force Base.

Eglin AFB

Eglin Field, Florida

Eglin Field near Valparaiso in the Florida panhandle was the training area for the Doolittle Raiders. Originally established in 1933 as the Valparaiso Bombing and Gunnery Range, the base was situated in a sparsely populated area only a short distance from the Gulf of Mexico. In 1937, the area was named Eglin Field in honor of Lt. Col. Fred T. Eglin, who died in an Alabama air crash earlier that year.

When an additional 800 square miles were ceded to it in 1940, the field was designated the Air Corps Proving Ground and became the site for gunnery training for fighter pilots as well as a major testing center for aircraft, equipment and tactics. The Doolittle Raiders spent three weeks training here from March 9 to 25, operating from Satellite Field 3 (Auxiliary Field 3). None of the buildings where the airmen lived and worked still stand.

Eglin is now the Armament Development and Test Center of the Air Force Systems Command.

Valparaiso Bombing and Gunnery Base in 1936. The following year the base became Eglin Field, named in honor of Lt. Col. Fred T. Eglin, who had been killed in an Alabama air crash.
Eglin AFB

The combination officer and enlisted mess, and quarters for permanent personnel at Eglin. This was one of three permanent buildings in 1938.
Eglin AFB

CHAPTER THREE
ON BOARD THE HORNET
DESTINY OF TASK FORCE 16

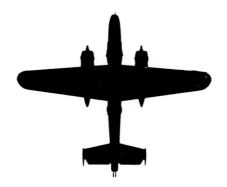

Shortly after the arrival of the *Hornet* in the Pacific, the carrier was ordered to Alameda Naval Air Station, near San Francisco, to load a group of B-25s. Twenty-two planes were available, but only 16 would fit on the flight deck. Some difficulty was encountered in loading the planes, but a large crane had accomplished the job by April 1. Seventy officers and 64 enlisted men went on board with the planes.

Original plans called for one of the 16 planes to be flown off by Lts. Dick Joyce and Hank Miller, as a demonstration for the other pilots. That plane was to return to the mainland. Doolittle and Capt. Marc Mitscher, however, decided that there would be a more-than-adequate take-off distance of 460 feet. The decision meant that one more bomber could be sent over Tokyo.

After Army aircrews went on board, they heard lectures on carrier deck procedures, safety precautions, naval customs and traditions, and shipboard living.

The *Hornet* left Alameda at 3 p.m. on April 1 and docked for the night at Berth 9 in San Francisco Bay. The next morning she sailed out and headed northwest, following the 40th parallel. The aircrews wondered why the ship departed on its secret mission in broad daylight in full view of thousands of Bay Area people. One reason was that the carrier's crew was still inexperienced—the Navy didn't want to risk a nighttime departure from a busy harbor whose tides were tricky.

Task Force 16.2 was built around the *Hornet*. It was composed of the cruisers *Nashville* and *Vincennes*, the oiler *Cimarron* and the destroyers of Destroyer Division 22, *Gwin*, *Meredith*, *Grayson* and *Monssen*. Capt. Marc Mitscher was in command.

Task Force 16.1 was built around the carrier *Enterprise* and would serve as an escort for the *Hornet*. It included the cruisers *Northampton* and *Salt Lake City*, the oiler *Sabine* and the destroyers of Destroyer Division 6, *Balch*, *Benham*, *Ellet* and *Fanning*. Adm.

William Halsey was in command.

Halsey's force left Pearl Harbor on April 7 and rendezvoused with Mitscher on April 12 at Latitude 38°00' North, Longitude 180°00'. With Halsey in overall command, the combined group—Task Force 16—then headed west toward the launch point 400 miles off the Japanese mainland.

Members of the ships' crews were not told of their destination until they were well out to sea, but they received the news enthusiastically. This seemed to be a chance "to pay back the emperor for Pearl Harbor."

With the *Hornet's* own planes stored away below the flight deck to make room for the B-25s, the Task Force relied on the *Enterprise* to provide air cover. The Navy was taking a great risk moving the ships so close to the enemy. Submarines, land-based planes or surface vessels could attack at any time, and inflict a blow that America could ill afford at this crucial moment of the war.

Relations between the *Hornet's* crew and the bomber airmen had been somewhat estranged until the announcement came of the impending attack on the Japanese homeland. After this B-25 crews received nothing but first-class treatment from their Navy hosts.

On-board training occupied aircrews' time. Navy Lt. Stephen Jurika, who had firsthand knowledge of Japan, delivered lectures that would be useful if crewmen were shot down in that country. Lt. T.H. White, the flight surgeon who would himself make the trip, lectured on first aid and sanitation. Cmdr. Frank Akers, the *Hornet's* navigator, conducted classes each day to hone the airmen's navigation skills. Akers supervised celestial navigation practice using star sights from the ship's deck as well as from the navigating compartments of the airplanes.

Doolittle himself lectured on targets and gunnery procedures. Gunners practiced on target kites flown from the carrier.

While the aircrews were put through their paces, the mechanics were going over the planes to make sure everything was in perfect order. Many small problems occurred and one engine had to be re-placed. Every B-25 was pronounced ready for action however.

Although their mission would be extremely hazardous, the aircrews had a carefree attitude and seemed to be little concerned over the dangers ahead. Many of them grew beards, shrugging off the suggestion that the Japanese might torture prisoners by plucking out facial hairs. Even so, a nagging question in the fliers' minds was what they should do if capture seemed imminent. Doolittle left this up to each individual, but he had decided he would crash his disabled plane into the most tempting target available.

As the task force approached the take-off point, the carriers were refueled and the oilers and destroyers released. During the night of the 17th, the remaining task force proceeded at 20-25 knots through dense fog, using radar to avoid collisions. In the morning hours of April 18, the fog lifted but low clouds hung over the ships and rain squalls were occurring frequently. The sea was rough, but everything was ready for the fast run to the launch point 400 miles off the Japanese coast.

Adm. William F. Halsey, commander of Task Force 16, at the time of the Tokyo Raid. USN (NH 85975)

USS Enterprise (CV-6), *flagship of the task force that escorted the* Hornet *to Japanese waters.*   USN (NH 67732)

USS Hornet (CV-8)

The carrier selected to carry the Doolittle Raiders to within striking distance of Japan was the *USS Hornet (CV-8)*. The ship, of the *Yorktown* class, was the first carrier ordered after treaty restrictions on total carrier tonnage were lifted. Launched in 1940 and commissioned in 1941, she trained her first air group in the Caribbean area in January 1942, and then returned to the Norfolk area to launch two B-25s from her flight deck in a feasibility test.

After her initial training, she left Norfolk for San Francisco in late March to load the 16 B-25s. Her secret cargo aboard, she rendezvoused with the carrier *Enterprise*, and launched the raiders on their historic mission on April 18.

The *Hornet* later fought in and survived the Battle of Midway and operations in the Solomon Islands, but she was sunk in the Battle of Santa Cruz in October 1942. Twenty-seven dive and torpedo bombers from the Japanese carriers *Zuikaku* and *Shokaku* scored six bomb and two torpedo hits, and two enemy aircraft made suicide crashes into the ship. In an effort to save the stricken vessel, she was taken into tow, but another airstrike, from the Japanese carrier *Junyo*, finished her. The decision was made to scuttle her, but it was an attack by two Japanese destroyers on the morning of Oct. 27, 1942, that finally sent her to the bottom.

Later in the war, a new carrier—the eighth of the Essex Class—was named *Hornet* in honor of the ship that launched Doolittle's raiders.

Displacement	20,000 tons
Length	809'
Width	83'
Draught	21' 9"
Aircraft	100
Crew	2,200

The USS Hornet (CV-8) *in 1941. Only months after carrying the raiders to their launch point, the 20,000-ton carrier was sunk at the Battle of Santa Cruz.*

USN (NH 81313)

TBD-1s on the flight deck of USS Enterprise. *The* Enterprise *provided the only air cover for the Task Force because the* Hornet's *aircraft had to be stored below deck to make room for the B-25s.*

Gunnery crews on board the Enterprise *practice as the Task Force heads into enemy waters.*

The destroyer Fanning *on escort duty with the task force.*   USN (#324218)

The Hornet *loaded with B-25s en route to launching point. The fighter overhead is an F4F from the* Enterprise.
                                                                            Gen. Knobloch (USN)

The Hornet *runs into rough weather on her way to the launching site. This photo was taken from the cruiser* Salt Lake City,
one of the escort vessels.
                                                                            Gen. Knobloch (USN)

When the task group was two days out of San Francisco, the Navy airship L-8 came out to drop B-25 parts to the Hornet.

USAF (#92992 Left, #92991 Right)

Crew #1 (Plane 40-2344). Left to right: Lt. Henry A. Potter (navigator), Lt. Col. James H. Doolittle (pilot), S/Sgt. Fred A. Braemer (bombardier), Lt. Richard E. Cole (co-pilot), S/Sgt. Paul J. Leonard (engineer-gunner).

USAF (#94600)

Crew #2 (Plane 40-2292). Left to right: Lt. Carl R. Wildner (navigator), Lt. Travis Hoover (pilot), Lt. Richard E. Miller (bombardier), Lt. William N. Fitzhugh (co-pilot), Sgt. Douglas V. Radney (engineer-gunner).

USAF (#94601)

Crew #3 (Plane 40-2270). Left to right: Lt. Charles J. Ozuk (navigator), Lt. Robert M. Gray (pilot), Sgt. Aden E. Jones (bombardier), Lt. Jacob E. Manch (co-pilot), Cpl. Leland D. Faktor (engineer-gunner). USAF (#94602)

Crew #4 (Plane 40-2282). Left to right: Lt. Harry C. McCool (navigator), Cpl. Bert M. Jordan (gunner), Lt. Everett W. Holstrom (pilot), Sgt. Robert J. Stephens (bombardier), Lt. Lucian N. Youngblood (co-pilot).

USAF (#94603)

Crew #5 (Plane 40-2283). Left to right: Lt. Eugene F. McGurl (navigator), Capt. David M. Jones (pilot), Lt. Denver V. Truelove (bombardier), Lt. Ross R. Wilder (co-pilot), Sgt. Joseph W. Manske (engineer-gunner).

USAF (#94604)

Crew #6 (Plane 40-2298). Left to right: Lt. Chase J. Nielsen (navigator), Lt. Dean E. Hallmark (pilot), Sgt. Donald E. Fitzmaurice (engineer-gunner), Lt. Robert J. Meder (co-pilot), Sgt. William J. Dieter (bombardier).

USAF (#94605)

Crew #7 (Plane 40-2261). Left to right: Lt. Charles L. McClure (navigator), Lt. Ted W. Lawson (pilot), Lt. Robert S. Clever (bombardier), Lt. Dean Davenport (co-pilot), Sgt. David J. Thatcher (engineer-gunner).

USAF (#94606)

Crew #8 (Plane 40-2242). Left to right: Lt. Nolan A. Herndon (navigator-bombardier), Capt. Edward J. York (pilot), S/Sgt. Theodore H. Laban (engineer), Lt. Robert G. Emmens (co-pilot), Sgt. David W. Pohl (gunner).

USAF (#94607)

Tom Griffin

Crew #9 (Plane 40-2303). Left to right: Lt. Thomas C. Griffin (navigator), Lt. Harold F. Watson (pilot), T/Sgt. Eldred V. Scott (engineer-gunner). Lt. James N. Parker, Jr. (co-pilot), Sgt. Wayne M. Bissell (bombardier).

USAF (#94608)

Crew #10 (Plane 40-2250). Left to right: Lt. Horace E. Crouch (navigator/bombardier), Lt. Richard O. Joyce (pilot), unidentified gunner, who was replaced at the last minute and did not go on mission, Lt. J. Royden Stork (co-pilot), Sgt. George F. Larkin, Jr. (flight engineer). The fifth member, S/Sgt. Edwin W. Horton, Jr. (gunner) is pictured in the insert.   USAF (#94609)

Crew #11 (Plane 40-2249). Left to right: Lt. Frank A. Kappeler (navigator), Capt. C. Ross Greening (pilot), Sgt. Melvin J. Gardner (engineer-gunner), Lt. Kenneth E. Reddy (co-pilot), S/Sgt. William L. Birch (bombardier).

USAF (#94610)

Crew #12 (Plane 40-2278). Left to right: Lt. William R. Pound, Jr. (navigator), Lt. Wiliam M. Bower (pilot), S/Sgt. Omer A. Duquette (engineer-gunner), Lt. Thadd H. Blanton (co-pilot), T/Sg. Waldo J. Bither (bombardier).

USAF (#94611)

Crew #13 (Plane 40-2247). Left to right: Lt. Clayton J. Campbell (navigator), Lt. Edgar E. McElroy (pilot), Sgt. Adam R. Williams (engineer-gunner), Lt. Richard A. Knobloch (co-pilot), Sgt. Robert C. Bourgeois (bombardier).

USAF (#94612)

Crew #14 (Plane 40-2297). Left to right: Lt. James H. Macia, Jr. (navigator-bombardier), Maj. John A. Hilger (pilot), S/Sgt. Jacob Eierman (engineer), Lt. Jack A. Sims (co-pilot), S/Sgt. Edwin V. Bain (gunner). USAF (#94613)

Crew #15 (Plane 40-2267). Left to right: Lt. Howard A. Sessler (navigator-bombardier), Lt. Donald G. Smith (pilot), Lt. (Dr.) Thomas R. White (gunner), Lt. Griffith P. Williams (co-pilot), Sgt. Edward J. Saylor (engineer).
USAF (#94614)

Crew #16 (Plane 40-2268). Lt. George Barr (navigator), Lt. William G. Farrow (pilot), Sgt. Harold A. Spatz (engineer-gunner), Lt. Robert L. Hite (co-pilot), Cpl. Jacob DeShazer (bombardier). USAF (#94615)

Air crews gather around Lt. Col. James Doolittle and Capt. Marc A. Mitscher, who are about to attach Japanese medals to a 500-pound bomb.

USN (NH 64472)

This well-publicized photograph shows Doolittle wiring a Japanese medal to the fin of a 500-pound bomb on the deck of the Hornet *before take-off for Tokyo.*   USAF (#51585)

Rising Sun medals attached to the fin of a Tokyo-bound bomb. The medals were a gift to Lt. Stephen Jurika, USN, from the Japanese government while he was a naval attaché in Tokyo, prior to the war. The medals were loaded on Doolittle's plane.   USAF

Crew members check the lashings of the bombers. The engines were covered to protect them from the weather.

Dwarfed by the B-25 bomber in the foreground. Navy fighters rest with folded wings on the edge of the Hornet's flight deck.

B-25Bs crowd the Hornet's *flight deck. The carrier could accommodate only 16 bombers if there was to be enough room to take off.*

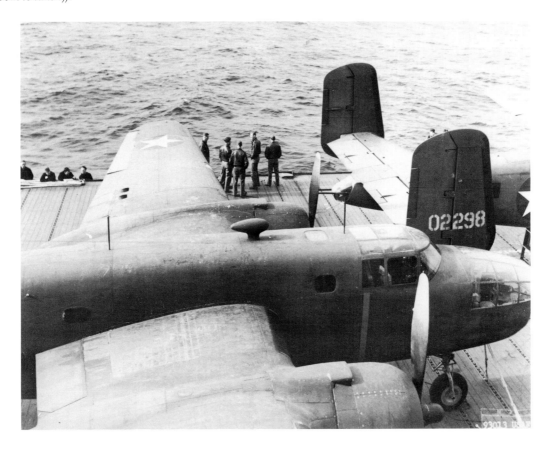

Looking out to sea, crew members stand beside their planes aboard the Hornet *en route to Japan.*

Escorts of the Task Force screen the Hornet *from possible enemy attack.*   USAF (#93001)

William Fitzhugh casts a thoughtful glance at a 500-pound bomb waiting on the elevator to be loaded aboard a B-25.   USAF (#92990)

As ship's crewmen watch, bomber crews load ammunition in preparation for the take-off.

Insignia of Plane #11 ("Hari Carrier"), one of the 16 bombers that took part in the raid.
USAF (Top #93008, Bottom #92731)

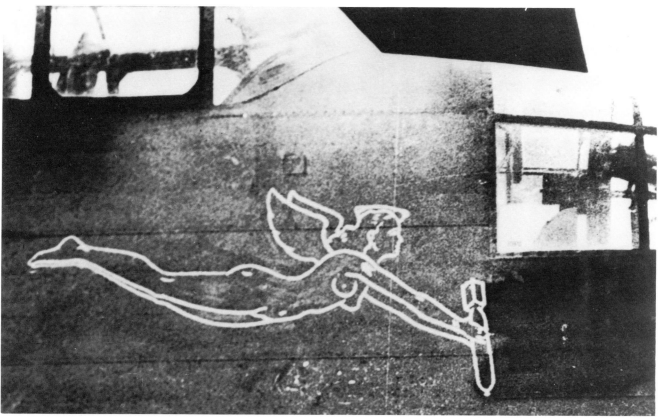

Lt. Henry L. Miller

Although he did not take part in the Tokyo raid personally, Lt. Henry L. Miller had a very important part in the successful completion of the operation.

He was born in the frontier gold camp of Fairbanks, Alaska, in 1912 and spent the first 17 years of his life there prior to entering the U.S. Naval Academy. He graduated in 1934. He spent the next three years on the battleship *Texas* followed by 34 years in naval aviation and various staff and shipboard assignments aboard aircraft carriers.

Miller was a flight instructor at Pensacola, Florida, in early 1942 when he received the assignment to proceed to Eglin Field, Florida, which was about 50 miles away, to teach a group of Army Air Force pilots how to take off from an aircraft carrier. From Eglin, he and Col. Doolittle flew to the West Coast and accompanied the crews aboard the *Hornet*. On April 18, 1942, Miller helped launch the 16 B-25s on their way to bomb Japan.

Following the Tokyo raid, Miller commanded Fighting Squadron 23 and Air Group 23 aboard the aircraft carrier *Princeton*, followed by Air Group 6 aboard the *Hancock*. On the last day of the was he was leading strikes on an electronics plant southeast of Tokyo.

After tours in the Pentagon, the Philippines, command of the *Hancock*, and other assignments, Miller was promoted to Rear Admiral in 1960. He was Assistant Chief of Staff for Plans, Commander-in-Chief Pacific, then Commander Carrier Division Three at the start of the Vietnam War.

In December 1965 while in the Vietnam area, he put the Navy's first Nuclear Powered Task Force, headed by his flagship the *Enterprise*, into Pentagon where he became Chief of Information for the Navy. His last tour of duty before retirement in 1971 was a Commander, Naval Air Test Center, Patuxent River, Maryland. Since retirement, Miller was involved in Real Estate and other ventures. He was an honorary member of the Tokyo Raiders Association.

Rear Admiral Miller was married to the former Lucille Dean of Opp, Alabama. They had two sons, Henry L. Jr. and Richard B.

Henry Miller died in 1993.

Commander Henry L. Miller, commander of Air Group 6, U.S.S. Hancock, 1944.

Rear Admiral H.L. Miller.   USN

CHAPTER FOUR
PLANNING AND DETECTION
ARMY PILOTS, MAN YOUR PLANES

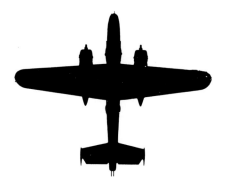

Planning

While the Doolittle raiders were being selected and trained in the United States, military planners in Washington and elsewhere were seeking possible landing sites for the B-25s after their secret mission had been completed. Russia seemed the best and closest haven, but the Kremlin was locked in a death struggle with Germany, and was not about to jeopardize her fragile neutrality with Japan by welcoming American bombers fresh from a Tokyo raid. Washington turned instead to China, and obtained permission for the raiders to put down at selected airfields around Chuchow, Chekiang Province, about 200 miles south of Shanghai, then refuel and fly on to Chungking, China's wartime capital deep in the interior. There, the planes and some of the airmen would be assigned to the newly organized Tenth Air Force for combat duty against the Japanese in China

and Burma. Some of the men would make their way back to the United States by various air routes.

The distance from Tokyo to Chuchow was 1,200 miles, just within the fuel capacity of a B-25 with extra gas and a launch site within 400 miles of Japan. Doolittle had calculated that the Chinese fields could be reached even from a 650-mile launch point, but that would leave no margin for error. It was agreed that if the U.S. task force were sighted or attacked before the raiders were in range of Japan, the B-25s would be launched to protect the fleet.

Other plans were set in motion. The submarine *Thresher* was sent into enemy waters from her Midway Island base to gather weather information and observe Japanese shipping.*

Washington was so concerned about word of the

---

*The *Thresher*, along with the *USS Trout*, was later put on patrol duty in the western Pacific to report any enemy surface forces that might jeopardize the secret mission.

mission leaking out to the Japanese that even the top allied military leaders were not fully advised. Generalissimo Chiang Kai-Shek, head of the Chinese government, was told about the mission but was not let in on all the details. He was very apprehensive—justifiably, as it turned out—about Japanese retaliatory measures against Chinese forces assisting the raiders. Even Col. Claire Chennault, leader of the Flying Tigers and organizer of an air warning net in China, was not fully briefed.

Complicating the situation was the very real possibility that the Chinese airfields might fall into enemy hands before the bombers arrived. Moreover, logistical problems plagued the preparations. Radio homing devices were supposed to guide the B-25s to each field, where fuel would be waiting, but neither the homing devices nor adequate amounts of fuel reached their destinations. In the end, it didn't matter—the bombers were launched a day early, and most never reached the fields anyway, because of fuel problems and weather conditions.

Doolittle's plan called for a takeoff from the *Hornet* at 6 p.m. on April 19. The landings were to be made in China no earlier than 4 a.m. the following day. Doolittle was to fly the first plane off the deck (assuming Gen. "Hap" Arnold would permit him to lead the mission) and would drop incendiaries over Tokyo to light the target for the rest of the bombers, which would take off about three hours later.

Once on board the *Hornet*, Doolittle brought out the intelligence files on possible targets in Japan and gave each crew the chance to choose its destination. Only military targets were to be hit; Doolittle stressed that civilian areas were to be avoided, and under no circumstances should the Imperial Palace in Tokyo be bombed. Targets included the industrial areas of Tokyo, Yokohama, Nagoya, Osaka, and Kobe, and the Yokosuka Naval Base.

The target decisions were not arrived at lightly. There would be only one opportunity to strike the enemy, and every bomb had to count.

Japan's Air Defenses

By early 1942 Japan controlled much of the Pacific. Her leaders were confident that no enemy force could or would attack their homeland, but they nonetheless had established a home defense force. Civil defense was stressed; anti-aircraft batteries ringed the major industrial cities. Several squadrons of Type 97 fighters were stationed on the mainland, and some carrier-based aircraft were off-shore. Most of Japan's carriers were stationed far from the homeland, however. One task force was returning from the Indian Ocean, but it would arrive too late to engage the raiders. Other naval

forces patrolled the coastlines, guarding against saboteurs and the remote possibility of an invasion.

As it turned out, Japan's defenses were totally surprised by the 16 American bombers. Few Japanese fighters challenged the raiders; at least two, and possibly three, others that did were shot down. One B-25 was hit by flak, but was not seriously damaged.

1st Lt. Yasuhide Baba pursued a B-25 with his Type 97 fighter. None of the bombers were downed by enemy fighters or anti-aircraft fire.   Dr. Yasuho Izawa, Japan

After the raid, Japanese air crews painted a white band around the red "meatball" on air defense fighters to distinguish the insignia from the American markings, whose white star contained a red ball.

Dr. Yasuho Izawa, Japan

Kawasaki Type 3 Ki-61 fighter planes such as this were stationed at Mito, northeast of Tokyo, at the time of the raid. Several chased the B-25s.

Dr. Yasuho Izawa, Japan

Detection

On the morning of April 18, the B-25 crews were making their final preparations for take-off on the following day. The planes, which had been spotted along the full length of the flight deck since the *Hornet* left Alameda, were now crowded aft, in take-off position. The ammunition had been loaded. Just before launch time, fuel tanks were to be topped off and personal gear loaded.

The first hitch in the plans came at 3:10 a.m. on the 18th, when the *Enterprise's* radar picked up what turned out to be a Japanese surface vessel. The American fleet changed course and avoided the enemy ship, but at daylight *Enterprise* air patrols sighted another vessel forty-two miles away. It seemed only a matter of time now before the entire task force would be spotted.

U.S. intelligence was not aware that the Japanese had stationed a fleet of fishing vessels on a picket line 600 to 800 miles off Japan to detect just such intruders as Task Force 16. Nor did the American forces realize that Japanese radio operators had been eavesdropping on the force, and had concluded that it was approaching the mainland with two and possibly three carriers. What the enemy didn't know, however, was that one of the flattops was carrying twin-engine bombers which had a much longer range and heavier striking power than did conventional carrier planes. The Japanese High Command figured that the fleet would have to sail within 300 miles of the coast to launch its planes. It was too early to become alarmed.

On the cruiser *Vincennes*, then on the *Enterprise's* right flank, Seaman Hubert B. Gibbons spotted a Japanese trawler just after daybreak only 12 miles away. The cruiser *Nashville* sank the enemy boat, but the damage had already been done. Intercepted Japanese radio messages indicated the trawler had reported the task force's position to the mainland.

Adm. Halsey acted quickly. He ordered the bombers to be launched immediately so that his fleet could turn back toward Hawaii and safety. His signalmen flashed a message to the *Hornet*: LAUNCH PLANES X TO COL DOOLITTLE AND GALLANT COMMAND GOOD LUCK AND GOD BLESS YOU.

On the deck of the *Hornet* everything began happening at once. Deck crews put the planes in final position and topped off the fuel tanks. Pilots and crewmen ran to their planes and started their take-off preparations. There was neither time nor room to store much more than bare essentials, but Lt. Jacob Manch managed to

get his portable phonograph aboard his plane and Dr. Tom White was able to distribute two pints of Navy rye to each airman.

Weather conditions were not ideal for a take-off. Gusty winds whipped up whitecaps on the rising swells, and rain spattered the flight deck. But there was no turning back—the fleet had come too far to give up now. Every pilot was acutely aware of the two white lines that ran the length of the flight deck on the port side. If he kept his wheels on the lines during take-off, his right wing would clear the carrier's island by six feet. Then the flier could worry about getting airborne. Though the pitching deck made take-off a tricky task, the 20-knot wind would give the planes lifting power. With luck and good piloting, the aircraft would have no trouble getting off the deck.

At latitude 35°43'N, longitude 153°25'E, 624 miles east of Tokyo, the take-off began at 8:15 a.m. ship's time, a day earlier than planned. The Task Force for some unexplained reason arrived at the launch point a day early.

Doolittle's was the first plane off the deck. The colonel took off just as the bow of the *Hornet* was rising. The pilot of the second plane, Lt. Hoover, kept his nose up too long and almost stalled. He managed to correct the mistake. After the third plane had taken off, Lt. Miller scrawled a chalkboard message directing the waiting planes to put their stabilizers in neutral. Smoother take-offs resulted. Lt. Lawson forgot to put his flaps down, but took off with no

Deck scene on the Hornet *during the launching of the B-25s on April 18, 1942.*   USN (NH53435)

problem. Three other planes began taxiing without their flaps down, but the deck crew caught them in time. Lt. Smith's plane received minor damage to its nose cone glass when it collided with the plane in front of it, but both planes made successful launches.

It was not until the 16th and final plane was being launched that misfortune struck. Seaman Robert W. Wall lost an arm when a gust of wind blew him into the idling prop. There was nothing anybody could do to prevent the accident, but it was unnerving to Lt. Farrow, the pilot, and his crew. They would have more bad luck when they bailed out over China.

After takeoff, each plane circled to the left and flew over the *Hornet*, aligning the ship's axis with the plane's drift sight to help establish an accurate navigational course.

Lt. Miller holding his chalkboard directing the remaining bombers to put their stabilizers in neutral for smoother take-offs.

U.S.S. Hornet's Log, April 18, 1942

Launching Course 300° true bearing 270° mi. distance 645 miles to Tokio.

03:30 G.Q.
07:30 Chow down
07:45 All hands to battle stations. Sighted enemy ships on horizon
08:05 U.S.S. Nashville open fire on enemy patrol boat
08:07 Prepared to launch planes.
08:15 First Army bomber left ship.
08:20 #2 (Enterprise launching planes.)
08:30 #3
08:32 #4
08:35 #5
08:37 #6
08:40 Enemy destroyer hit directly by U.S.S. Nashville, listing badly and afire. (#7.)
08:47 #8
08:52 #9
08:55 #10
09:00 #11
09:01 #12 Visibility very poor. Ship heading into storm.
09:02 #13
09:05 #14
09:10 #15
09:16 #16 Tokio bound. Man lost arm in propeller of last bomber.
09:21 U.S.S. Nashville sunk second enemy ship. ship headed out of danger zone
10:25 False alarm. No action on radar pickup of enemy planes.
12:15 False alarm. No action on radar pickup of enemy planes. (chow)

12:55 Musical programs from Tokio still being received.
13:27 Musical programs from Tokio still being received. Army bombs expected to reach Tokio at 14:15.
13:50 Unidentified plane dist. 25 mi.
13:59 Plane belong to Ent.
14:00 All low frequency radios going off the air in Tokio
14:09 All low frequency radios going off the air in Tokio with news.
14:12 Third enemy ship sighted on horizon
14:15 All radio stations in Tokio off the air.
14:16 U.S.S. Nashville contacts enemy ship.
14:17 U.S.S. Nashville and two planes following ship bombing and firing.
14:20 Jap hoist white flag. Nashville takes prisioners and sinks ship. Score 3-0 favor the Yanks.
14:30 Administry of propoganda for home consumption from radio. Tokio states enemy bombers appeared over Tokio just before noon today and inflicted heavy damage on schools and hospitals in the first raid of the war. The Japanese people were highly indignant.
14:40 Bombs being dropped on starboard side, target unknown, believed to be sub.
14:50 Army bombers got through o.k. Some reported shot down. Osaki, Nogoya, and Tokio bombed.
18:10 From Capt. to Crew.---
The captain wishes to commend the officers and men of the U.S.S. Hornet on their alertness, efficiency and willingness in their first taste of real action. It is due to this that our first engagement was a complete success.
18:20 Darken ships
18:30 Secure.

I Sighted
An Enemy Vessel

An account of my experiences on April 18, 1942, when I was a Yeoman 1st class in charge of the forward battle lookout station on the U.S.S. VINCENNES, escorting the U.S.S. HORNET on the now famous "Tokyo Raid."

Our Task Force, the U.S.S. HORNET and the U.S.S. ENTERPRISE, steaming in line, flanked port and starboard by four cruisers, the U.S.S. VINCENNES (our ship) being stationed on the starboard bow of the Hornet, and another cruiser on the port bow, and two other cruisers stationed port and starboard quarter of the Enterprise. There were three destroyers forward of our box formation, and three others forming a screen astern. With this tight formation, we were steaming at flank speed, directly Westward, with Lt. Colonel James H. Doolittle and his squadron of B-25 bombers nested on the flight deck of the Hornet.

At approximately 45 minutes before daylight "Battle Stations" was sounded, and all hands took their stations for dawn alert, a period when it was most critical for a surprise attack by an enemy force.

I took my station in charge of the forward battle lookout station, in a closed compartment immediately above the navigation bridge. This compartment was shielded by heavy protective armor plating, with only slots through the armor shield, four slots port and four starboard, with strong binoculars fixed in each slot. Beneath each slot was a stool fixed into the deck, and within each slot the lookout could rotate his binoculars to cover an area of about 20 degrees. Lookouts were trained to report anything ob-

served that was not part of our task force. This morning I had cautioned the lookouts to be especially observant since we were only about 800 miles east of Tokyo, and 200 miles from the proposed launch site for those birds nested on the flight deck of the Hornet (all hands had long since been informed of the destination of those birds).

Practically all the lookouts were youngsters, seamen second class, and our ship never having experienced actual combat action, it was difficult for them to conceive the gravity of our present situation. One lad, only a few months in service, was more prone to want to rest his eyes than the others, had been warned twice for taking his eyes from his binoculars to rest, and upon the third occasion when he backed away, dropped his head down to rest his eyes, I became much concerned. I grasped him by the collar and belt, lifted him from his stool and shoved him back across the station and assumed his place. The first thing I saw, looking across to the port and across the bow of the Hornet and ahead of the cruiser stationed on her port bow, was the masthead and cross arm of a vessel, not a part of our task force. I immediately opened the circuit of my telephone, and started talking, giving the sighting with relative bearing and approximate range. My telephone was connected with the navigating bridge, and the flag bridge on the same level as the navigation bridge, and when I started talking the flag bridge talker started repeating the alarm, and signalmen started running up a flag signal to our task force, giving the message. Almost immediately the cruiser on the Hornet's port bow directed her guns on the bearing given and opened fire. The target just exploded.

—*Hubert B. Gibbons*
Paducah, Kentucky

The starter gives a B-25 the readiness signal on a flight deck pitching in turbulent seas.   USAF (#41194)

The starter "hits the deck" as a bomber rolls toward her take-off. All 16 bombers took off successfully.
USAF (#41195)

One of the bombers has taken off from the flight deck and is heading for Japan.

USN (#41197)

Lt. Richard Knobloch took this photograph of a Japanese boat in enemy waters after the bomb run over Yokasuka.

Leaving the Hornet *flight deck behind this B-25 bomber climbs into the overcast sky.*

With heavy seas and overcast sky, a B-25 bomber takes off on the last leg of its journey to Japan.

CHAPTER FIVE
THE MISSION
RETURNED TO JAPAN WITH INTEREST

The B-25s found clearer weather as they approached the Japanese mainland, and began forming into five 3-plane flights as much as possible. The flights were at a very low altitude and spread over a 50-mile front, to make the attack more difficult to defend and to give the impression that the raid involved more than only 16 bombers. Soon Doolittle's B-25s were flashing over a variety of Japanese targets. The surprise was complete.

The first flight, led by Lt. Hoover, bombed northern Tokyo; the second, led by Capt. Jones, hit central Tokyo; the third, led by Capt. York, bombed the southern part of the city and the Tokyo Bay area; the fourth, led by Capt. Greening, struck Yokohama and the Yokasuka navy base; the fifth, led by Maj. Hilger, hit Nagoya and Kobe.

Minimal anti-aircraft fire and fighter resistance was encountered. As the B-25s raced along at nearly tree-top height, the Americans could see Japanese farmers working in the fields and villagers going about their daily chores. Never having seen Ameri-

can planes, the Japanese assumed the bombers were their own.

One bomber was hit by flak, but was not damaged seriously. The raiders encountered few enemy aircraft, and when they did they successfully defended themselves. Lt. Joyce's plane shot down several Japanese fighters, and three others were listed as probable from Watson's and Greening's planes.

All the B-25s dropped their bombs on target except Lt. Holstrom's plane, which was one of the few that did encounter stiff fighter opposition. Holstrom was forced to jettison his bombs into the ocean.

Though the raids hardly impeded Japan's capacity to make war, they did inflict damage to many military and industrial targets. In Tokyo, bombs damaged power plants, magazines, steel works, chemical works, a gas company, power stations, oil tank factories, a truck plan and a warehouse. In Yokohama, the targets were docks, warehouses, an oil refinery and oil tanks. At the Yokosuka naval base, bombs pounded the dock area and what was thought to be a partially completed aircraft carrier. At Nagoya, a barracks, oil storage warehouses and the Mitsubishi aircraft factory were blasted. In Kobe, the bombs hit the industrial area, docks and an aircraft factory.

Eleven B-25s hit their primary targets, four hit secondary targets and only one was forced to jettison its bombs.

At 12:30 p.m., Kay Tateishi, a newsman for Japan's official Domei News Agency, was standing on a railway platform in Central Tokyo when he saw "a couple of unfamiliar planes, flying low."

"It looked like some daring maneuver," he recalled. "A commuter nearby said, 'It looks real, doesn't it? Just like a foreign aircraft breaking through Japanese air defenses. I guess the Imperial forces want to impress the people that they are fully prepared.' Then the planes released their bombs and the people became frightened. Someone shouted, 'Hey, that's real enemy bombing!' "

The Japanese accused the Americans of hitting schools and civilian areas, and charged that 50 civilians were killed or wounded. A Tokyo newspaper, the *Asahi Shimbun,* called the raid "an inhuman, insatiable, indiscriminate bombing attack on the sly."

Japanese defense authorities soon began receiving bomb damage reports. Some 90 buildings had been destroyed, including Mitsubishi Heavy Industrial Corporation Factory No. 1 of the Japanese Steel Corporation, the Japanese Diesel Manufacturing Co., a warehouse of the Yokohama Manufacturing Co., the Nagoya aircraft factory, an army arsenal and naval ammo dump.

Even though Doolittle had stressed that only military targets were to be attacked, it was inevitable that some non-military targets would be hit. Fifty civilians were reported killed and 250 wounded.

Japanese propagandists described the bombings as indiscriminate and wanton, and charged that the Americans strafed civilian targets. Newspapers reported that Japan's defense efforts had been gallant, but in truth the military had been taken completely by surprise and very few of the home defense aircraft had risen to challenge the bombers. While there had been some intense anti-aircraft fire, it had been largely ineffective. The altitude of the fire was accurate, but the bursts had fallen behind the American aircraft, possibly because the gunners did not realize the speed of the B-25s. A few barrage balloons were situated in the Tokyo area, and they diverted an attacking plane to its secondary target.

This enemy defense was summed up in a confidential American intelligence report written after the raid:

> *The overall picture was one of inadequate defense. The warning system did not appear to function; interception by fighters was definitely cautious; and anti-aircraft fire, responding slowly, did not reach the intensity one would expect for so important a city as Tokyo.*

When the bombers had completed their runs, they headed south for China. One, piloted by Capt. Greening, took time to shoot up an enemy trawler on his way. But gas consumption was a major concern and the airmen had little time for such diversions. Even if the fuel held out, the pilots would have a difficult time finding their landing strips, especially as it would be dark by the time they neared China.

Ski York's plane was having particular problems. Unauthorized carburetor adjustments at Sacramento had caused the engines to use up alarming amounts of fuel. There was no chance of reaching China— York headed the plane north toward Siberia, which seemed preferable to a ditching in the Pacific. After many hours in the air, the crew spotted an airfield 40 miles north of Vladisvostok, and landed there uninvited. The five airmen were interned in Russia for 13 months before they finally escaped into Iran and made their way back to the United States.

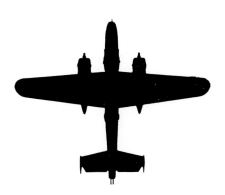

Fighters from the Enterprise *provide an umbrella for a climbing B-25.*   Gen. Knobloch (USN)

York's plane just coming in for a landing at the airfield north of Vladisvostok, Siberia.

Tokyo Raid map showing the course of the B-25s and signed by most of the survivors of the mission.

Donated by Mrs. M. B. Ireland, Dallas, Tex.

This map of Japan and China was autographed by members of the Air Corps crews on board the Hornet before the raid.

AFM

As all the planes were lost after the Tokyo raid, only two photos taken over Japan survive. These were snapped by Lt. Richard A. Knobloch, co-pilot of Plane #13 (Lt. Edgar E. McElroy, pilot). Top photo shows the naval base at Yokosuka. Bottom photo is another view of Yokosuka, possibly a barracks area. USAF (Top #93022, Bottom #93021)

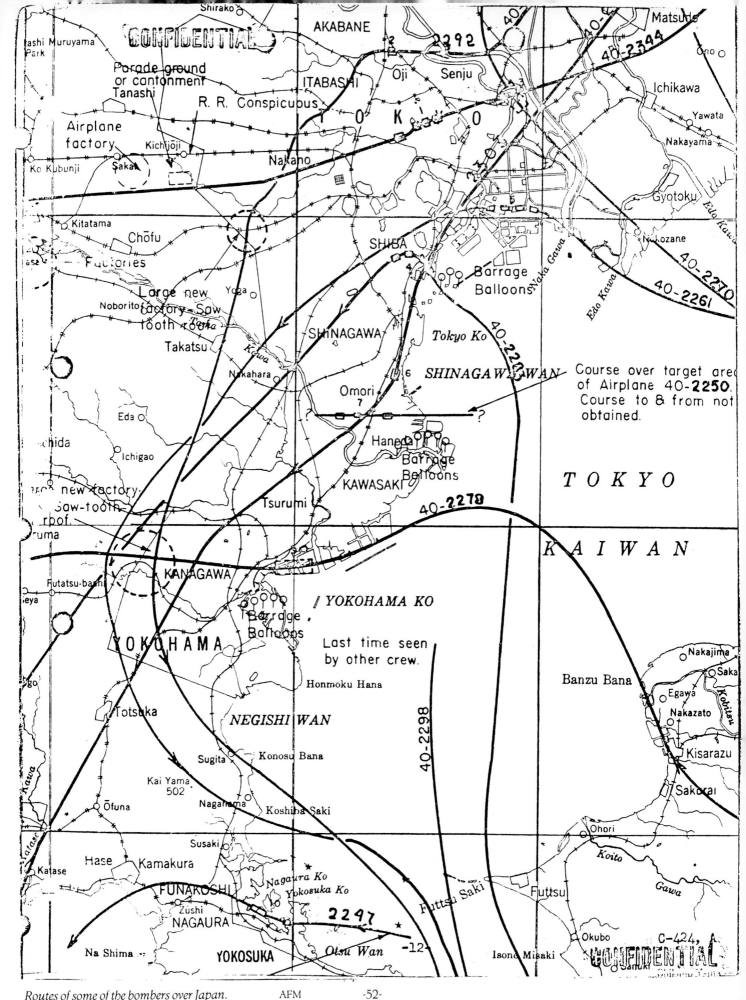

Routes of some of the bombers over Japan.   AFM   -52-

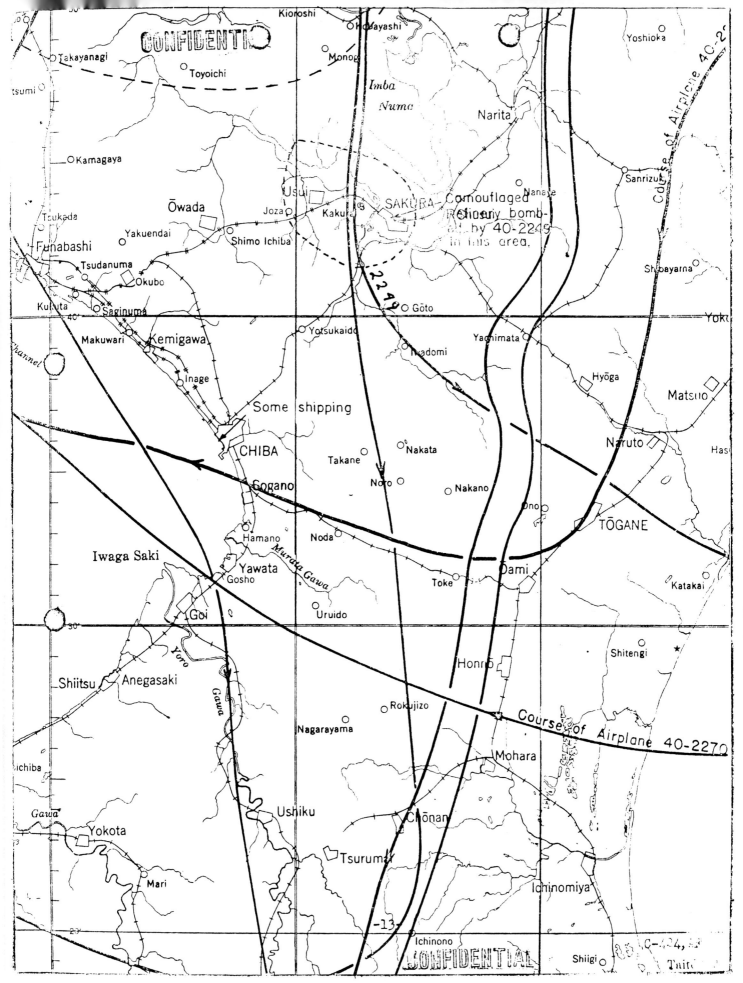

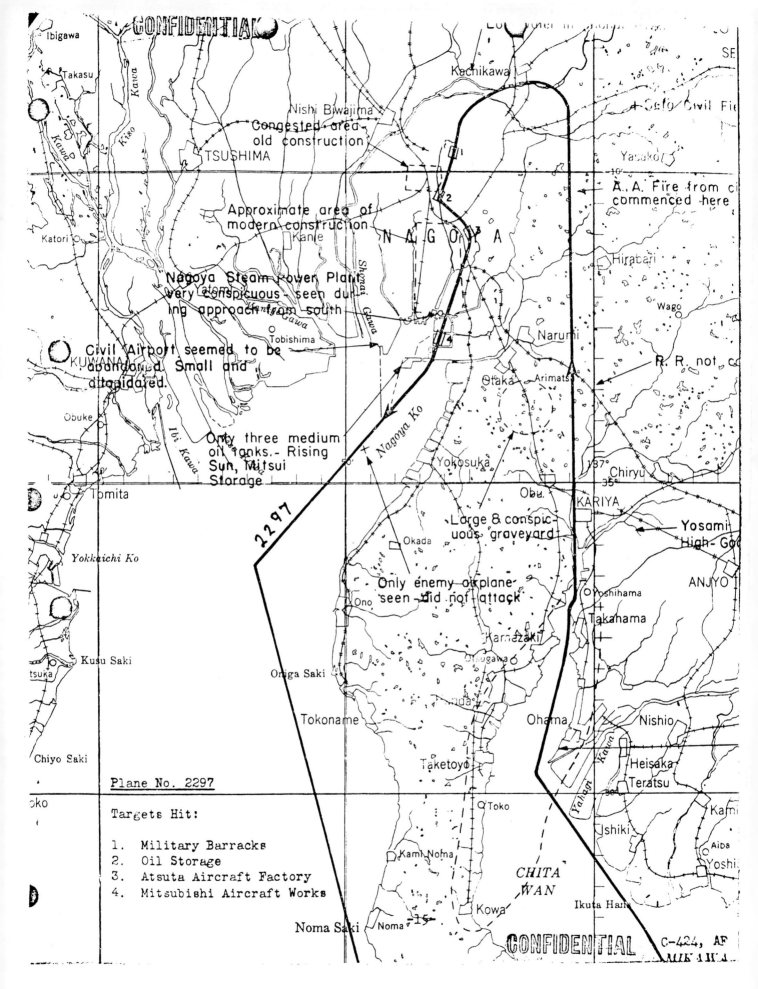

Ibigawa

Takasu

Kiso Kawa

Kawa

Nishi Biwajima

Congested area
old construction

TSUSHIMA

Kachikawa

Seto Civil Fie

Yasako

A.A. Fire from ci
commenced here

Approximate area of
modern construction

Kanie

N A G O Y A

Hirabari

Katori

Wago

Nagoya Steam Power Plant
very conspicuous - seen during approach from south

Shonai Gawa

atsu
Gawa

Tobishima

Narumi

Civil Airport seemed to be
abandoned. Small and
dilapidated.

KUWANA

Otaka

Arimatsu

R. R. not c

Obuke

Nagoya Ko

Ibi Kawa

Only three medium
oil tanks.- Rising
Sun, Mitsui
Storage

Yokosuka

Chiryu

137°

Obu

KARIYA

Yosami
High- Go

Tomita

Okada

Large & conspic-
uous graveyard

ANJYO

Yokkaichi Ko

Ono

Only enemy airplane
seen did not attack

Yoshihama

Takahama

Kusu Saki

Kamezaki

Otsugawa

Ohama

Nishio

Origa Saki

Yahagi Kawa

Heisaka

Teratsu

Chiyo Saki

Tokoname

Taketoyo

Ishiki

Kami

Aiba

oko

Toko

Yoshi

Plane No. 2297

Targets Hit:

1. Military Barracks
2. Oil Storage
3. Atsuta Aircraft Factory
4. Mitsubishi Aircraft Works

Kami Noma

CHITA
WAN

Kowa

Ikuta Han

Noma Saki

Noma

2297

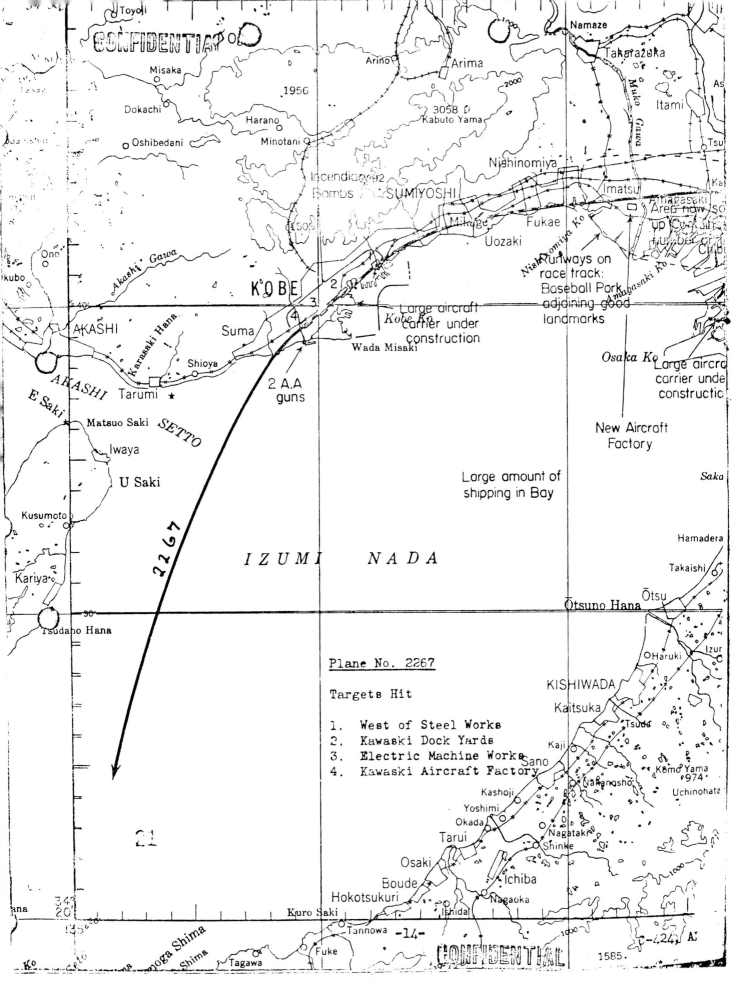

Toyo̅l
Misaka
Dokachi
Harano
Oshibedani
Minotani
.1956
Arino
Arima
3058 D
Kabuto Yama
2000
Namaze
Takarazuka
Muko Gawa
Itami
Tsu
As

Nishinomiya
Imatsu
Amagasaki
Area now so
up Currents
number c?

Incendiary
Bombs SUMIYOSHI
(1500)
Mikage
Fukae
Uozaki

KOBE
Akashi Gawa
AKASHI
Suma
Karasaki Hana
Shioya
Tarumi
SETTO
Matsuo Saki
Iwaya
U Saki
Kusumoto
Kariya
E Saki
Ono
kubo
Tsudaho Hana
ha
Kuro Saki

Kobe Ko
Wada Misaki
Large aircraft
carrier under
construction
2 A.A
guns

Nishinomiya Ko
Amagasaki Ko
Runways on
race track:
Baseball Park
adjoining good
landmarks

Osaka Ko
Large aircra
carrier unde
constructio

New Aircraft
Factory

Large amount of
shipping in Bay

Saka

IZUMI NADA

Hamadera
Takaishi
O̅tsu
O̅tsuno Hana

Plane No. 2267

Targets Hit

1. West of Steel Works
2. Kawaski Dock Yards
3. Electric Machine Works
4. Kawaski Aircraft Factory

KISHIWADA
Kaitsuka
Tsuda
Kaji
Sano
Kashoji
Yoshimi
Okada
Tarui
Osaki
Boude
Hokotsukuri
Ichiba
Nagaoka
Ishidal
Nakanosho
Komo Yama
974
Uchinohata
Nagataki
Shinke
O Haruki
Izur

21

Tannowa
Fuke
Tagawa
Shima
ga Shima

1000
1585

C-24 A

Japan Times & Advertiser

MORNING EDITION

MORNING EDITION

Incorporating
The JAPAN CHRONICLE and The JAPAN MAIL

No. 15,461   (THE 17th YEAR of SHOWA)   TOKYO, SUNDAY, APRIL 19, 1942   Price 15 Sen

9 ENEMY RAIDERS DOWNED

Japanese Annihilate Remnants in Cebu; Passi Is Captured

Ensign of Imperial Navy Flies Over Iloilo, Panay Isle

U.S. LOSSES HUGE

CEBU CITY, April 18—Launching an offensive early Thursday morning, Japanese Forces by yesterday completely mopped up enemy remnants in the hilly area around Sayao, 20 kilometers north of the City of Cebu.

The Japanese forces closed in from three directions, while air units effected severe bombing raids upon the approximately 1,600 enemy troops which took to a vantage point of the hill and attempted to resist.

Unable to hold their own owing to the severe Japanese onslaughts from air and land, the enemy troops retreated in utter confusion into the hinterland, leaving 300 dead. Many prisoners were captured, includ a battalion commander.

JAPANESE BOMB ENEMY IN CEBU

AT A JAPANESE BASE IN THE PHILIPPINES, April 18—Closely cooperating with land units operating on the Cebu Island, squadrons of the Japanese Army Air Force yesterday violently bombed enemy troops entrenched in the hilly areas northwest of Cebu City. Another wave of Japanese Air Force the same day intensively dive-bombed enemy positions on the Panay Island in parallel with the Japanese columns which are expanding their spheres of operations on the island.

PASSI CAPTURED BY JAPANESE UNITS

PANAY, April 18—The vanguard of the Japanese Forces which occupied Iloilo captured Passi, 45 kilometers north of Iloilo yesterday morning, pursuing enemy remnants fleeing northward.

The Japanese residents who have been reportedly interned at Passi are believed to have been taken elsewhere.

JAPANESE ENSIGN FLIES OVER ILOILO

ABOARD JAPANESE WARSHIP, April 18—The ensign of the Imperial Navy was hoisted for the first time in the port of Iloilo, Panay Island, at 3 p.m. yesterday by a fleet of Japanese warships, which had collaborated with Army Units in their successful landings at three different points of the island of army.

With numberless scattered islets, the waters surrounding the island of Panay have been regarded as submarine bases of the enemy.

As a result of the Japanese occupation of the island, however, communications with the various islands rapidly will be restored.

U.S. ADMITS HUGE CAPTIVE LIST

LISBON, April 17—Colonel Henry L. Stimson, United States Secretary of War, announced today that American captures taken by the Japanese in Bataan number 16 officers and 60,000 civilians and soldiers, while 68 troop remnants and nurses escaped to Corregidor before the fall of the peninsula, it is reported here from Washington.

Fearing public reaction, the American War Department originally had announced that Lieutenant-General Jonathan M. Wainwright's forces included 12,000 Americans and 24,000 Filipino soldiers, but War Secretary Stimson's latest revelation doubles these figures.

This effort to couch American troop numbers in an automatic confession of the complete rout suffered by Lieutenant-General Wainwright and his men in Bataan.

GLOUCESTER IN NEAR EAST

Brother of British King to Inspect West Africa Forces

BUCHAREST, April 17—The Duke of Gloucester, brother of King George VI of Gera, Britain, has arrived at a certain British base in the Near East to inspect West Africa on an inspection tour of the British troops stationed there, it was announced today by a special correspondent of the British War Ministry.

The objective tour by the Duke of Gloucester is being made at the initiative of Major-General Claude F. Auchinleck, Commander-in-Chief of the British forces in the Middle East.

Restricts Civilian Evacuation

LONDON, April 18—The German evacuation of Ireland Province directed either their particular public conversation from English public conversation are prohibited except by special permission of military and municipal authorities of a city, according to a Reuter despatch from London today.

NEW STATE POLICY OUTLINED BY PIBUL

Responsibility of Maintaining Independence Rests on People, Says Premier

AUTARCHY EMPHASIZED

Development of Industry to Point Where Nation May Become Exporter Hoped

BANGKOK, April 18—With the recent session of the Assembly as a background, Premier Pibul outlined the morning house a four point statement clarifying the Government's policy and explaining the present situation in Thailand under the War of Greater East Asia.

It is the duty of all of each people of this country to share the responsibility for maintenance of independence and in strengthening national defense, he pointed out, and fulfilment of this obligation in maintenance of the full observation of the duty to cooperate with Thailand's Allied countries for a final victory of the War.

Independence of Thailand is the only guarantee of the outbreak of the War.

Emphasizing the need of the land's self-sufficiency, the Premier expressed the national desire to provide to help such a stage so as to able to export industries in the future.

In conclusion, he emphasized the necessity to pay special attention to the requirement of national mobilization and nation, pointing out that case of Thailand depends much upon national efforts.

DUTCH BELATEDLY APPROVE MACARTHUR'S APPOINTMENT

Political Circles in London Give No Importance to Move Adopted

LISBON, April 16—Commenting on the announcement made by the refugee Nether-lands Government in London of its recognition of the appointment of General Douglas MacArthur as commander-in-chief of the Combined Allied Forces in the Southwestern Pacific, political observers here a permanent disunity among the Allies in the delayed announcement.

The same circles also pointed out that the Netherlands have been practically all of the possessions in East Asia, its recognition of General Douglas MacArthur as commander-in-chief of the Southwestern Pacific has little authority, especially in view of the fact that the Dutch Government is only of nominal existence.

U.S. RUBBER PLANT SET UP

Goodyear Tire Company to Build Factory in Peru

BUENOS AIRES, April 16—The American Government today announced that it has given permission to the Goodyear Tire Company to establish a plant for the manufacture of tires and tubes as well as other rubber manufactures, according to a Reuter's News Living Arrangements have also been made for reconstruction of Chile-house Harbor, about 180 kilometers north of Lima, under the supervision of an American harbor specialist, Frederick Sears, the dispatch added.

Two Vessels Sunk

VICHY, April 16—The sinking of two American and one Swedish freighter was announced by the United States Navy Department today, a Havas dispatch from Washington revealed. The three were fully equipped with State Secretary, but how the vessels were sunk.

Declines U.S. Invitation

BERLIN, April 17—The Chilean Ambassador to the United States has informed the U.S. State Department that Barton Jaran, newly appointed Chilean Foreign Minister, "regrets that he cannot accept the United States Government's invitation to visit Washington because he is fully occupied with State functions," the German News Agency reported from Washington today.

Imperial Family Absolutely Safe In First Air Raid Over Capital

Not a single enemy plane flew over the Imperial Palace during Saturday's air raid. That the Kashikokoro, the sanctuary of the Imperial Palace, remained absolutely secure, according to Domei, is a matter to be congratulated upon by the 100,000,000 people. His Majesty the Emperor attended to State affairs as usual while the air raid was going on. His Imperial Majesty received in audience Home Minister Michio Yuzawa at 2 p.m. and listened to a report submitted by the Home Minister. That Her Majesty the Empress, Her Majesty the Empress Dowager, His Imperial Highness the Crown Prince, His Imperial Highness Prince Yoshi, all other members of the Imperial Family and all other Princes and Princesses of the Blood are quite safe also must be mentioned with awe, reports Domei.

Premier Hideki Tojo went to the Imperial Palace at 6.05 p.m. Saturday and after writing down his name on the Book of Visitors, withdrew. Home Minister Yuzawa again was received in audience by His Imperial Majesty at 5.20 p.m. on the same day and submitted to the Throne relevant reports. After 4 p.m. on the same day, Foreign Minister Shigenori Togo, Navy Minister Shigetaro Shimada, Communications Minister Ken Terashima, Welfare Minister Michiyo Iwamura, President of the Planning Board Lieutenant-General Teiichi Suzuki, Koki Hirota, General Baron Sadao Araki, both of whom are accorded the treatment of their previous Cabinet posts, and many other important officials went to the Imperial Palace to offer congratulations on the safety of the Imperial Family. They all recorded their names on the Book of Visitors.

Foreign News Spotlight
Exclusive Flashes

ANTI-BRITISH FEVER RISES IN U.S.

STOCKHOLM, April 18—The greatest obstacle to Anglo-American cooperation is the increasing anti-British sentiment which he encountered everywhere during his tour of the United States, declared the special correspondent of the London Daily Express.

The Life magazine, a leading American pictorial weekly, openly expressed antipathy toward the British for their faulty war efforts, the correspondent reported. "Today," he continued, "the people in the United States entertain much less cordial feeling toward the Englishmen than before the outbreak of the war in the Pacific on December 8, 1941. The somewhat more friendly attitude shown by the Americans during Churchill's visit suffered a dangerous set-back after British reverses at Singapore, Libya and the recent successful passage of German warships through the English Channel. This ill-feeling cannot be improved easily by a few victories."

AUSTRALIAN LABOR SHORTAGE ACUTE

SAIGON, April 18—Costly drains upon Australian manpower in the disastrous campaigns of Malaya, Singapore, and Java and the heavy losses in the earlier fighting in Greece, Crete and North Africa have imposed a tremendous burden upon available men in the Commonwealth to create a dearth in labor.

According to the Australian Broadcasting Company report intercepted here, 60,000 men and 40,000 women are required to fill the gaps in industrial labor which have been taxed by the blanket conscription measures for the Australian army, militia and defense corps. Army Minister Ford announced yesterday that men over 45 years, who have been exempted from compulsory service, would be called to serve in the labor corps in a move to meet the shortage.

British-Chiang Friction

CANTON, April 17—Eloquently reflecting the increasing friction between British and Chungking forces on the Burma front, The National Herald, Chungking news-paper, in its editorial Wednesday, declared that the lack of uniformity in the Allied command was the cause of the Allied fiasco in the Burma campaign, it was learned here today.

DOG-FIGHTS STAGED IN AIR OVER CAPITAL

Army Machines Intercept and Shoot Down Invading Enemy Planes

BARRAGE BALLOONS UP

Anti-Aircraft Batteries Greet Hostile Craft With Fierce Fire

For the first time in history Tokyo was visited by hostile planes on Saturday, says Domei.

The attack came at 12.30 p.m. The invading planes dropped explosive and incendiary bombs at a number of places.

As soon as the enemy appeared over the capital, Army planes rose in their clean and in actual dog fights more than were shot down.

The antiaircraft batteries were active. They met the invaders with a barrage of fire.

Barrage balloons were sent up in the area of the approach of enemy planes to the capital.

Fire fighters, members of the defense corps and volunteer firemen, members of neighborhood associations, rose to their work of extinguishing fires which were raised by the enemy.

LOCAL SOVIET RAIDS REPULSED BY REICH

German Aircraft Bomb Harbor Installations in Attack Over Southampton

BERLIN, April 17—German forces yesterday repulsed a number of local attacks by Soviet troops in the central and northern sectors of the Eastern Front, the High Command announced today.

The Luftwaffe launched air raids against Soviet rear communications lines and airfields yesterday, inflicting considerable losses to the Soviets in aircraft and material, the communique said.

Referring to the battle of Britain, the communique said combat German fighter planes that down 11 British aircraft over the Channel and the southern coast of Britain.

German bombers were said to have raided supply plants in Southampton, causing explosions and confla-gration.

Night Raid Britain

BERLIN, April 18—German fighter bombers on Friday night conducted attacks on war important targets on the British Isles according to an announcement by German military quarters.

Eleven were reported on harbor installations at Southampton and large fires were caused. In an extensive over the British Isles last night, German fighters shot down 11 British airplanes.

SILK BODY REORGANIZED UNDER FOUNDATION SETUP

The Dai Nippon Silk Association, holding the 37th general meeting at the Sanjo Kaikan, Marunouchi, from 3 p.m. Friday, changed the present structure of corporate body from that of a foundation. The Association authorities decided to make a readjustment the name of Foundation Dai Nippon Silk Association by merging into the Foundation Silk Scientific Research Institute. The reorganization has been made from the standpoint of contributing to the enforcement of the duties to strengthen and simultaneously in view of the prevailing situation of the silk industry.

Damage By Incendiary Bombs Small; Planes Repulsed

WARNINGS SOUNDED

The following communique was issued by the Eastern District Army Headquarters at 2 p.m. on April 18:

"Enemy planes, coming from several directions, attacked the Keihin district at about 12:30 p.m. today. The invaders, counter-attacked by our air and ground defense forces, are in gradual retreat. The enemy planes so far ascertained to have been shot down number nine. The damage suffered by us seems to be slight. The Imperial Family is in absolute security."

KOBE, NAGOYA FIRES UNDER CONTROL

Fires caused by enemy incendiary bombs which were dropped in Nagoya and Kobe were brought under control, the Central District Army Headquarters announced at 4 p.m. Saturday.

1. In the vicinity of Nagoya, incendiary bombs were dropped at six places, however, fires are now almost under control.

2. In Kobe, one incendiary bomb each was dropped in Prefecture, and farm village in Wakayama Prefecture, however, no damage was caused.

ENEMY PLANES OVER NAGOYA, KOBE

The following communique was issued by the Central District Army Headquarters at 2 p.m. on April 18:

1. Two enemy planes raided Nagoya at about 1:30 p.m. today. Bombs were dropped, but the damage done was slight.

2. One enemy plane raided Kobe at about 2:05 p.m. It dropped incendiary bombs. The damage done was not serious.

The time has come for the people to put up a determined fight to make sure of defending the air with success.

AIR, LAND DEFENSE UNITS ACTIVE

The following communique was issued by the Eastern District Army Headquarters at 4.30 p.m. on April 18:

1. It is a matter of congratulation to us that the Imperial Family is safe.

2. The corps guarding the air was very prompt to locate the enemy planes, with the result that the air raid alarm could be sounded in time.

3. Thanks to the efforts of the air and land defense units and presence of mind and quick action of the people, the damage inflicted by the invading planes could be limited to the minimum. The individual people are asked to be further prepared for the prevention and extinction of fires.

4. The invaders dropped some explosive bombs. The bombs used by them for the most part were of the incendiary. It seems that the incendiary bombs dropped by the enemy planes were of the two kilogram type. There is no warrant in dreading such bombs. These missiles sometimes lodge under the ceilings after penetrating roof tops. The people are asked to be on their guard.

5. The Army Air Defense Corps has for the first time actually met the enemy. The morale of the members is very high. They are adopting stricter measures to prepare them to meet the enemy in the future.

6. The deepest sympathy is expressed to the families of the victims of the raids and to persons who sustained injuries in the attacks.

RAID WARNING LIFTED IN KANTO

The air raid warning in the Kanto and Tokai districts was lifted Saturday afternoon, reports Domei. The precautionary air raid warning, however, is in effect at present in these two districts.

TOKAI, EAST AND NORTH KINKI

According to an announcement by the Central District Army Headquarters, an air raid warning was issued in the Aichi district and the Tokai district, i.e. the main Kinki district and in the north Kinki district on April 18.

CHUGOKU AND SHIKOKU DISTRICTS

An air raid warning was issued for the Chugoku and Shikoku districts on the afternoon of April 18, according to an announcement by the Central District Army Headquarters.

TOHOKU AND HOKKAIDO DISTRICTS

An air raid warning was issued in the Tohoku and Hokkaido districts on the morning of April 18, according to Domei. Shortly after a precautionary warning was issued in the Kanto district.

KYUSHU AND WESTERN CHUGOKU

An air raid warning was issued in south and north Kyushu in the afternoon of April 18 according to a telephone message to Domei from Fukuoka. Shortly afterward the air raid alarm was sounded in the western part of the Chugoku district.

PRECAUTIONARY WARNING IS SOUNDED

A precautionary warning was issued in the area under the jurisdiction of the Central District Army Headquarters at 4 p.m. on April 18, according to an announcement by the Headquarters.

A precautionary warning was issued in the entire area under the jurisdiction of the Western District Army Headquarters on April 18, according to Domei.

The day after the raid, the Tokyo English-language newspaper, Japan Times and Advertiser, *contained propaganda about the raid. Of course, no planes were lost over Japan.*

AFM

CHAPTER SIX

EXPERIENCE IN CHINA

LUSHU HOO MEGWA FUGI (I AM AN AMERICAN!)

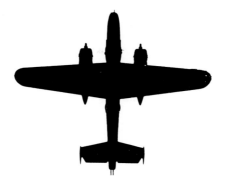

The raid was over but much adventure still lay ahead for the 15 crews heading into China.

Fuel was getting low, night was falling and the weather was getting worse. Relying chiefly on their instruments, the pilots tried to find their way to air-fields around Chuchow, approximately 100 miles in-land from the Japanese-controlled coastline. Having been airborne for up to 15 hours, the crews were ex-hausted and tense.

As the airfields had no homing devices or landing lights, nightfall virtually assured that each plane would have to crash-land or be abandoned in the air. The crews could not even be certain they were over friendly territory.

Of the 15 B-25s that made it to China, 11 were aban-doned in flight, their crews bailing out, and four crash-landed or ditched off the Chinese coast. Two fliers died in crash landings; one was killed after bail-ing out.

Most of the crewmen were eventually picked up by Chinese peasants or guerrilla bands and treated with the utmost kindness when it was learned they were Americans. They were welcomed as heroes for inflicting damage on the hated enemy.

As the fliers were secreted through the countryside away from Japanese-occupied territory, they were regarded as a curiosity by the peasants, many of whom had never seen a white person before.

One crew was turned over to the enemy by Chinese who were working for the Japanese. In most cases, however, the Chinese people showed great respect for the Americans and went out of their way to help them escape. Thousands were to pay with their lives for this help in the days and weeks afterward.

Soon the Japanese would begin a three-month ground and air assault on the province of Chekiang, where some of the crews had landed. The assault prompted Chiang Kai-shek to send the following

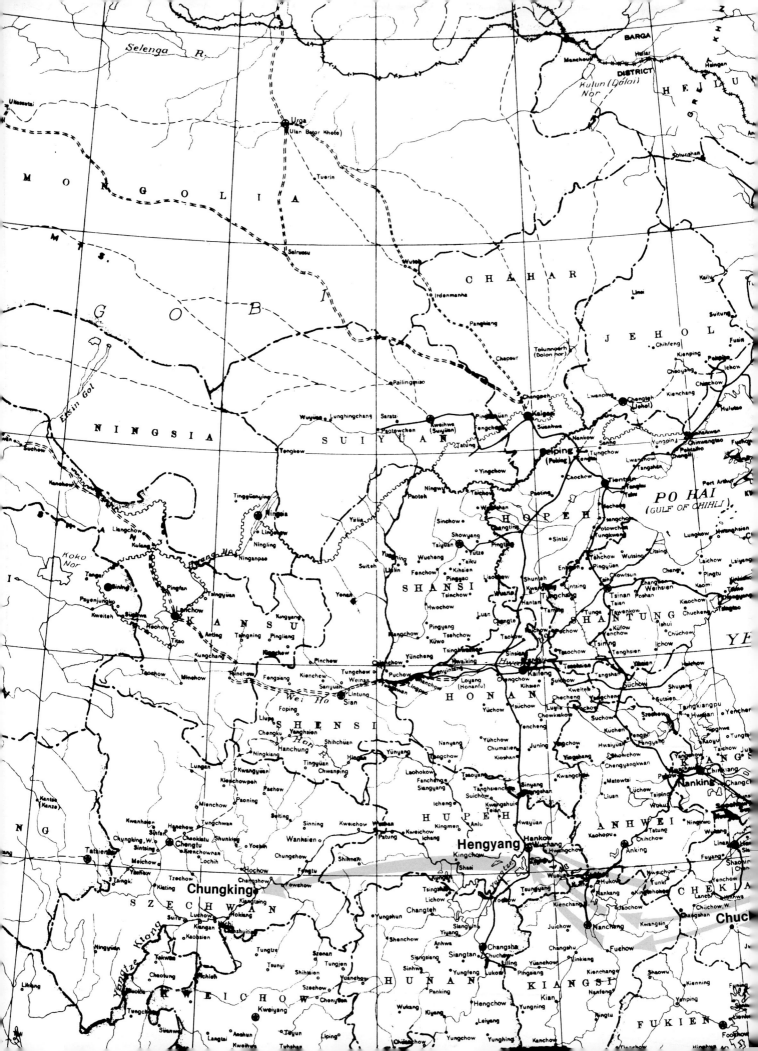

JAPAN, CHINA, SIBERIA
APRIL 1942

APPROXIMATE ROUTE
OF ONE B-25

APPROXIMATE ROUTE
OF FIFTEEN B-25s

SCALE

| 100 | 50 | 0 | 100 | 200 |

MILES

-N-

Tokyo
Yokohoma
Nagoya
Kobe
Osaka

J A P A N   S E A
(NIHON HAI)

EAST CHINA SEA
(TUNG HAI)

J A P A N

SHIKOKU

RYUKYU

ISLANDS

SEA
(HAI)

Wreckage of Doolittle's plane which crashed north of Chuchow. Chinese soldiers are examining the wreckage. AFM

Col. Doolittle sits by a wing of his downed bomber the day after the raid. The Chinese had already stripped the plane of equipment that could be used against the Japanese. Photo was taken by S/Sgt. Paul Leonard, one of the crewmen.

USAF

cable to the United States:

AFTER THEY HAD BEEN CAUGHT UNAWARE BY THE FALLING OF AMERICAN BOMBS ON TOKYO, JAPANESE TROOPS ATTACKED THE COASTAL AREAS OF CHINA WHERE MANY OF THE FLYERS HAD LANDED. THESE JAPANESE TROOPS SLAUGHTERED EVERY MAN, WOMAN AND CHILD IN THESE AREAS—LET ME REPEAT—THESE JAPANESE TROOPS SLAUGHTERED EVERY MAN, WOMAN AND CHILD IN THOSE AREAS, REPRODUCING ON A WHOLESALE SCALE THE HORRORS WHICH THE WORLD HAD SEEN AT LIDICE...

The Japanese forces penetrated 200 miles into China, wiped out entire villages, razed American church missions and destroyed the airfields around Chuchow. Perhaps as many as 250,000 Chinese, most of them civilians, were killed. Chiang's fears of a Japanese retaliatory raid were realized.

Parasol-carrying Chinese soldiers salvaged whatever they could from the wrecked planes.   USAF (#25758)

Here are brief accounts of what happened to each of the 16 crews:

Crew #1, pilot Doolittle: Bailed out about 70 miles north of Chuchow. Col. Doolittle located his crew and his crashed B-25 the next day. From the house of the governor of Chekiang Province, the Colonel sent this message to Gen. Hap Arnold: TOKYO SUCCESSFULLY BOMBED. DUE BAD WEATHER ON CHINA COAST BELIEVE ALL AIRPLANES WRECKED. FIVE CREWS FOUND SAFE SO FAR. His crew and some others eventually made it to Chungking, but Doolittle was ordered back to the United States on May 5 before knowing the fate of all his crews.

Crew #2, pilot Hoover: Crash-landed near Ningpo on the Chinese coast without injury to crew members. The airmen were picked up by Chinese guerrillas and transported west to Chungking, arriving there on May 14. The crew was helped by Tung-Sheng Liu.

Crew #3, pilot Gray: Bailed out over Chekiang Province. Cpl. Faktor died of injuries received during his parachute landing. Rest of crew made it to Chuchow with the help of Chinese guerrillas. With other B-25 airmen, the crew was taken to Hengyang and then Chungking.

Crew #4, pilot Holstrom: Bailed out safely over Chekiang Province some 40 miles south of Shangjao. Chinese peasants and soldiers guided them to Chuksien, Hengyang and Chungking.

Crew #5, pilot Jones: Bailed out safely over Chekiang Province. Crew members were treated like heroes by the Chinese as they were moved from one city to another. At Chuksien, they were reunited with other B-25 airmen. Eventually got to Hengyang and Chungking.

Crew #6, pilot Hallmark: Ditched just off the Chinese coast. The impact threw the pilot through the windshield, injuring him. Two crew members, Sgt.

S/Sgt. Jacob Eierman, injured during his parachute landing, looks up from his cot to permit a picture with Chinese friends. Maj. John Hilger, pilot of Plane #14, is behind Eierman. USAF (#B-25757)

Sgt. Eldred Scott was caught in a tree on the edge of a cliff after bailing out. He stayed there until daylight the next morning.

William Dieter and Sgt. Donald Fitzmaurice, were so seriously injured that they drowned before reaching shore. The three remaining fliers were captured by the Japanese four days later and taken to Shanghai. Hallmark was later executed; Meder would die in prison, Nielson survived his prison ordeal and was released at the end of the war.

Crew #7, pilot Lawson: Ditched off the Chinese coast. The four forward crew members were propelled through the windshield and nose of the plane. Sgt. David Thatcher helped to get the injured companions safely ashore. Lawson was the most injured, and eventually had to have his leg amputated by Lt. Thomas White of Smith's crew. Despite many harrowing days and several close calls, the crew managed to elude the Japanese and reach friendly territory. Lawson would later recount the adventure in *Thirty Seconds Over Tokyo*, a book that was subsequently was made into a popular Hollywood film.

Crew #8, pilot York: After a successful bomb run, York concluded that his rapidly dissipating fuel supply would not get him to the Chinese coast, so he headed the plane toward Russian Siberia. After landing 40 miles north of Vladivostok, however, the airmen were interned by the Russians, who were not at war with Japan. The Americans lived at various internment sites in Russia, but eventually were sent to Ashkhabad near the Persian border. With the help of a Russian citizen, they escaped into Persia (Iran) and made it back to the United States in May 1943, 13 months after the raid. One of the crew members, Robert Emmens, recounted their adventures in a book, *Guests of the Kremlin*.

Crew #9, pilot Watson: Bailed out 100 miles south of Poyang Lake, farther inland than any other B-25. Watson dislocated his shoulder badly enough to require surgery when he returned to the United States. The crew members were helped by Chinese civilians

Several raiders are led through a friendly Chinese village. From left are Lt. Macia, Lt. Sims, S/Sgt. Eierman and Col. Hilger. The Japanese took revenge on the Chinese for helping the Americans escape. It was estimated that more than 250,000 Chinese, most of them civilians, were killed in the areas where the planes crashed.   USAF (#25759)

AIRPLANE MODEL B-25 B **A.C. NO.** 40 2242 **ORGANIZATION** B-25 Prod. Det. **STATION** U.S.S. Hornet **DATE** 4-18-42

INSPECTION STATUS				AIRPLANE AND ENGINE TIME RECORD (ENTER IN HOURS AND MINUTES)						SERVICING AT STATION OF TAKE-OFF (CHECK IMMEDIATELY BEFORE TAKE-OFF)											
	DATE OR HOURS DUE	INSPECTED TODAY		ENGINE	NO. 1	NO. 2	NO. 3	NO. 4			FUEL (GALLONS)		OIL (QUARTS)								RADIATOR CHECKED
		BY	STATION						SERVICE		SERVICED	IN TANKS	NO. 1		NO. 2		NO. 3		NO. 4		
				HOURS TO DATE	150:25	150:25							SERV.	IN TANKS	SERV.	IN TANKS	SERV.	IN TANKS	SERV.	IN TANKS	
PREFLIGHT	3/18/42			HOURS TODAY	8:50	8:50			1ST	1130			140		140						
DAILY	3/16/42			TOTAL	159:15	159:15			2ND												
25 HOURS	174:50			OIL CHANGE DUE	Eng Change				3RD												
50 HOURS	199:50			CYNO. CLEANING DUE	141:50	199:50			4TH												
100 HOURS	247:50			HOURS TO DATE			150:25		5TH												
				AIRPLANE HOURS TODAY			8:50														
				TOTAL			159:15														

STATUS TODAY

EXPLANATION: R Eng. Overspeeds 50 RPM.

INSTRUCTIONS FOR PILOTS AND MECHANICS

PILOTS: EACH PILOT WILL PRINT NAME AND RANK BELOW, AND INDICATE "OK" OR, IF ANY DEFECT OR MALFUNCTIONING OCCURRED, EXPLAIN THE TROUBLE.

MECHANICS: TRANSPOSE "TOTAL FLIGHT TIME" FROM FORM 1 TO ENTRIES "HOURS TODAY" UNDER "AIRPLANE AND ENGINE TIME RECORD" ABOVE. PRECEDE EACH REMARK WITH THE NAME OF THE STATION. EXPLAIN ANY RED SYMBOL ENTERED UNDER "INSPECTION OF AUXILIARY EQUIPMENT". ENTER ANY MAINTENANCE WORK DONE WHILE AIRPLANE IS ON THE FLYING LINE OR AWAY FROM ITS HOME STATION. SIGN EACH REMARK MADE.

EXCEPTIONAL RELEASE

WHEN THE "STATUS TODAY" IS INDICATED BY A RED SYMBOL AND AN "EXCEPTIONAL RELEASE" HAS NOT BEEN GRANTED BY AN AUTHORIZED ENGINEERING OFFICER, THE PILOT OF THE AIRPLANE WILL SIGN THIS RELEASE BEFORE FLIGHT.

RELEASED FOR FLIGHT

INSPECTION OF AUXILIARY EQUIPMENT

EQUIPMENT	SYMBOL	INSPECTED BY	STATION
BOMBARDMENT			
GUNNERY			
NAVIGATION			
RADIO			
OXYGEN			
PHOTOGRAPHIC			
CHEMICAL			

WAR DEPARTMENT AIR CORPS FORM NO. 1 A TENTATIVE - SEPT. 1940

FLIGHT REPORT - ENGINEERING

REDIFORM—PAT'D.—AMERICAN SALES BOOK CO.,INC.,NIAGARA FALLS, N.Y.

Flight report of Capt. York, who landed in Russia after the Tokyo attack. He kept it throughout his 13-month internment.

USAF (#92980)

and soldiers, and two Catholic missionaries, Fathers Dunkis and Moore. After a short stay in Ihwang, the airmen were taken to Nanchang, Hengyang and Chungking.

Crew #10, pilot Joyce: Bailed out safely near Chuchow, Chekiang Province. With the help of Chinese civilians and soldiers, the airmen made it to Chuksien a week later, and then to Chungking.

Crew #11, pilot Greening: Bailed out near Chuchow, Chekiang Province. Sgt. Gardner sprained his ankle badly. The crew was escorted by Chinese farmers to a river and eventually to Chuksien and Chungking.

Crew #12, pilot Bower: Bailed out near Chuchow, Chekiang Province. Sgt. Duquette suffered a broken foot. The airmen were escorted to Chuchow and then to Chungking.

Crew #13, pilot McElroy: Bailed out safely near Poyang. The airmen landed within three miles of the Japanese forces, but were not detected. They were taken to Poyang by Chinese soldiers. Later they were escorted across Poyang Lake and on to Chuchow, then bused to Hengyang and flown to Chungking.

Crew #14, pilot Hilger: Bailed out southeast of Shangjao. Hilger was injured but could walk; the other crew members escaped injury. They were taken to the ancient city of Kuang Feng and paraded through the streets as heroes. On April 20, they reached Shangjao and then moved on to Chuchow, where they witnessed several Japanese air raids. After joining Doolittle and other airmen in Chuchow, the crew traveled to Hengyang, where most of the B-25 crews had assembled by May 3. That group was then flown to Chungking to be decorated. There, the airmen would be returned to the United States or reassigned to units in India or China.

Crew #15, pilot Smith: Ditched off the Chinese coast, all crew members safe. The plane remained afloat for eight minutes, giving the crew time to retrieve some gear. This proved to be very important, because it permitted Lt. Thomas White to locate the medical bag and supplies that helped save Lt. Ted Lawson's life. The crew managed to stay just ahead of searching enemy soldiers, and eventually made it to safety at Chuchow. From there the airmen proceeded to Hengyang and Chungking.

Crew #16, pilot Farrow: Bailed out south of Poyang Lake near Nanchang. All crew members were captured by the Japanese in the next few days. Farrow and Spatz were executed; Barr, Hite and DeShazer were imprisoned for 40 months in Japan and China, then freed at the end of the war.

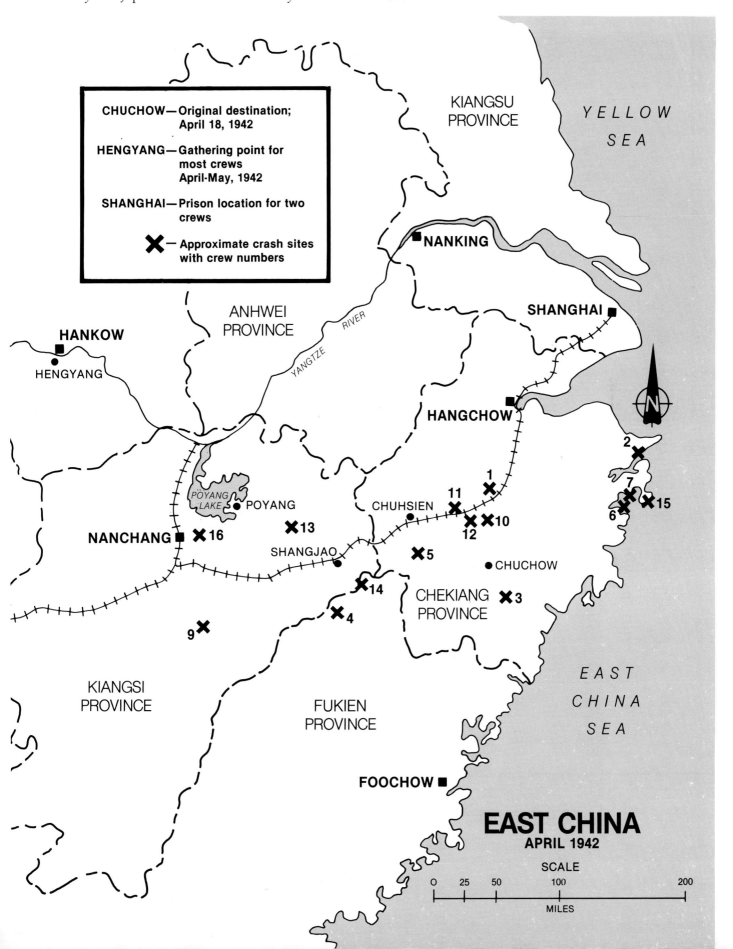

CHUCHOW—Original destination; April 18, 1942

HENGYANG—Gathering point for most crews April-May, 1942

SHANGHAI—Prison location for two crews

✗ — Approximate crash sites with crew numbers

KIANGSU PROVINCE

YELLOW SEA

ANHWEI PROVINCE

YANGTZE RIVER

NANKING

SHANGHAI

HANKOW

HENGYANG

HANGCHOW

POYANG LAKE

POYANG

NANCHANG ✗ 16

CHUHSIEN

✗ 1

✗ 11

✗ 12 ✗ 10

✗ 2

✗ 7

✗ 6 ✗ 15

✗ 5

SHANGJAO

✗ 14

✗ 4

✗ 9

CHEKIANG PROVINCE

✗ 3

CHUCHOW

KIANGSI PROVINCE

FUKIEN PROVINCE

EAST CHINA SEA

FOOCHOW

EAST CHINA
APRIL 1942

SCALE

0   25   50   100   200

MILES

Tung-Sheng Liu

Liu was an English-speaking aeronautical engineer who, just before the raid, had escaped from Shanghai into unoccupied territory to take an aircraft factory job. He happened to be in the area when Travis Hoover's crew was picked up by guerrillas, acted as an interpreter for the Americans, and helped guide them on their journey to Chungking. He also assisted Ted Lawson's crew members after they reached Chuksien.

Born in 1917, Liu graduated from National Tsing Hua University.

The raiders regretted leaving Liu behind, but he survived the war and then managed to get to the United States to do graduate study. He received an M.S. in aeronautical engineering in 1947 from the University of Minnesota, and spent the next nine years working at the university. From 1956 to 1978 he was employed by the U.S. Air Force at Wright-Patterson AFB in Ohio. He became a United States citizen in 1954, and is now retired in California. Liu is an honorary member of the Toyko Raiders Association.

Tung-Sheng Liu, Huntington Beach, California.

Chinese villagers gawk at downed American airmen. Some of the natives had never seen a white man before. USAF (#C-25757)

A group of Tokyo Raiders pose outside a shelter carved into a mountainside. They lived here for 10 days, waiting for an opportunity to reach Allied territory.
USAF (#C-25758)

This U.S. Air Force photograph was entitled "From Aerial Umbrella to Chinese Parasols." It shows the crew of Plane #13 and unidentified Chinese soldiers. Crew members, from left, are Lt. Clayton Campbell, Sgt. Adam Williams, Lt. Edgar McElroy and M/Sgt. Robert Bourgeois. Lt. Richard Knobloch took the picture. The Americans were on their way to safety after having bailed out.

USAF (#A-25759)

Chinese use native conveyances to transport American airmen down from the mountains in which their B-25 had crashed. USAF (#A-25757)

Doolittle and his crew with Chinese officials. From left, S/Sgt. F.A. Braemer; S/Sgt. Paul Leonard; Chao Foo Ki, director of the Branch Government of Western Chekiang Province; Lt. Dick Cole; Doolittle; Henry H. Shen, bank manager; Lt. Hank Potter, and General Ho, secretary of the Western Chekiang Province Branch Government. USAF (#92990)

Doolittle and his crew with Chinese friends at the National Culture Institute. NASM (#82-957)

Members of Plane #2 with officials somewhere in China after crash landing. From left, Lt. Carl Wildner; Mr. Chu, district commissioner; Lt. William Fitzhugh; Lt. Travis Hoover; Tung-Sheng Liu, interpreter; Lt. Richard Miller; and Sgt. Douglas Radney.   AFM

所待招軍空陽術團務服地戰會員委事軍
二九一念紀士勇軍空謝美京東炸轟次首待

Some of the Tokyo Raiders assemble before leaving China for the United States or other war theaters. The Chinese inscription says, "Air Force Reception, Department of Military Affairs Committee of the War Zone Unit of Heng Yang, greeting the American Air Force Heroes who made the first bomb raid on Tokyo."
Gen. Knobloch

Several Raiders at a farewell gathering with Chinese friends. Americans, from left in top photo, are Sgt. Edward J. Saylor; Lt. Thomas R. White; Lt. Don Smith; Lt. Griffith Williams; and Lt. Howard A. Sessler. In bottom photo, a paper sign in background proclaims, in English, "UNITING OF ALL DEMOCRACIES WILL OVERCOME THE AXIS POWERS!" USAF (Top #94599, Bottom #2788)

-71-

Father William Glynn

Father William Glynn arrived in China in 1939 as a Catholic missionary. In 1940 he took charge of a mission and school at Ying Tan, and assumed supervision of 15 smaller missions in the area. A few days after the Tokyo raid, Lt. McElroy and his crew were brought to Father Glynn, who gave them refuge for a few days before they were put on a train for Chuchow. Doolittle and some 20 other Raiders also visited the mission and were helped on their journey westward.

Angered by the assistance given the American fliers, the Japanese overran the mission in June. Glynn and other priests were forced to hide in the mountains for more than a month, until an outbreak of dysentery in the Japanese Army prompted their withdrawal. Before leaving, the Japanese burned the mission and town, and killed thousands of civilians.

Father Glynn became an auxiliary chaplain with the U.S. Air Force in China and stayed in the country until 1948, when he returned to the U.S. on his first vacation in nine years. The Communist takeover prevented him from returning to China. He spent the next few years in St. Louis, Chicago and New Orleans, and now lives in San Antonio, Texas, where he is an auxiliary chaplain at Kelly and Lackland air bases.

Father William Glynn, San Antonio, Texas.

Bishop Charles Quinn and Father Tom Smith of Vincentian Foreign Missions, in a hideout in the Chinese hills. They sought shelter here because the Japanese were taking revenge on those who helped Tokyo Raiders who had crashed nearby. AFM

Madame Chiang Kai-Shek decorates James Doolittle with the Order of Yung-Hui, 3rd Class, and John Hilger with the Order of Yung-Hui, 4th Class, at Chungking on April 29, 1942. Doolittle had just been promoted to brigadier general. USAF (#58933)

Three Doolittle Raiders receive a medal and a thanks from Madame Chiang Kai-Shek in Chungking. From left are Roy Stork, Richard Knobloch, wearing his patch from the 37th Bombardment Squadron, and Clayton Campbell. Gen. Knobloch

Several Raiders pose with a B-25 called Obliterators Excuse Please *at an airfield in China on Sept. 18, 1942, five months to the day after the famous raid.*   USAF (#73997)

Eight Raiders celebrate at an American air base in China. From left are Sgt. Douglas Radney, Sgt. Edwin Horton. Capt. Horace Crouch, Lt. Jack Manch, Maj. Everett Holstrom, Lt. William Fitzhugh. Lt. Lucian Youngblood and Capt. Clayton Campbell.   AFM

美國空軍健將揚威三島紀念

衡陽市市長朱玖瑩敬贈

鵬程萬里

A Chinese scroll presented to Doolittle in commemoration of the Tokyo raid.

NASM

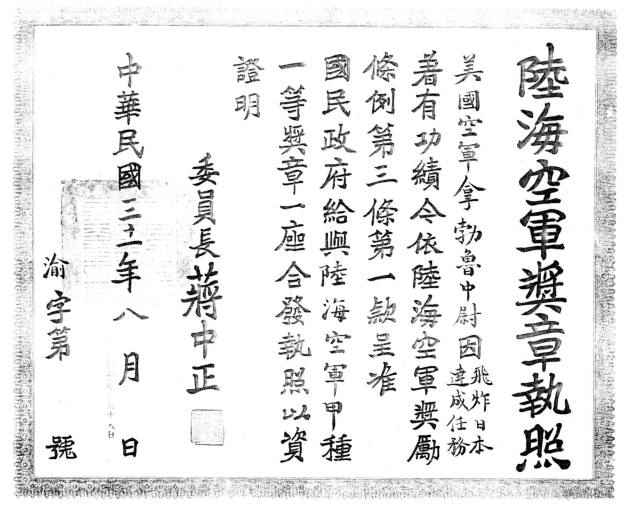

This certificate of award from the Chinese Army, Navy and Air Force, with the approval of the Chinese government, was sent to the Raiders a few months after the raid. According to Title 3, Article 1, which deals with awards of the Army, Navy and Air Force, it presents first class recognition to the American airmen for their successful bombing mission over Japan. It was issued at Chungking on Aug. 18, 1942, under the name of Chaing Kai-Shek. Gen. Richard Knobloch

The Captured Crews

Eight raiders from two crews were captured by the Japanese. Lt. Dean E. Hallmark, Lt. Robert J. Meder and Lt. Chase J. Nielsen became prisoners after Hallmark ditched his plane in the surf along the Chinese coast. Two crew members, Sgt. William Dieter and Sgt. Donald E. Fitzmaurice, drowned after the ditching.

Lt. William G. Farrow and his crew (Lt. Robert L. Hite; Lt. George Barr; Cpl. Jacob D. DeShazer and Sgt. Harold A. Spatz) bailed out near Japanese-occupied Nanchang and were captured by enemy troops within a day or so.

When Doolittle learned about the two captured crews, he offered a reward or ransom for their return, and he tried to persuade the Chinese army to rescue them. Nothing came of his efforts however; four of the airmen would spend the next 40 months as prisoners-of-war;* three would be executed; one would die in prison.

The eight captured airmen eventually were taken to Tokyo. They were interrogated and tortured for many weeks, and each eventually was forced to sign statements that they had committed crimes against Japanese civilians. They were then taken back to Shanghai to await their fate.

The Japanese had decided to make an example of their captives and conduct a trial. The verdict was decided before the proceeding had begun. Only the punishment was undetermined. The court condemned Hallmark, Farrow and Spatz to death. The five others were sentenced to life imprisonment.

The executions were carried out at the Kiangwan Military Prison, Shanghai, on Oct. 15, 1942. Lt. Meder died on Dec. 1, 1943, the victim of dietary deficiencies in the military prison at Nanking, where

---

*Japan was not a signator to the Geneva Convention for the treatment of prisoners-of-war.

the five other airmen had been transferred.

In August 1945, a daring group of OSS men parachuted into Peking and successfully negotiated with the Japanese for the release of the four remaining prisoners, who had been secretly moved there from Shanghai.

Torture, solitary confinement and inadequate food had taken their toll on the survivors. Though weak and emaciated, DeShazer, Hite and Nielsen were well enough to be flown to Chungking and eventually back to the United States. George Barr was too sick to travel; it would be many months before he would return to a normal life.

Four of the Japanese officials responsible for the treatment and execution of the raiders were brought to China after the war and put on trial. Capt. Sotojiro Tatsuta, warden at the Kiangwan Prison and executioner of the three airmen, Lt. Gen. Shigeru Sawada, commanding general of the Japanese Imperial Thirteenth Expeditionary Army, and Lt. Yusei Wako and Capt. Ryukei Okada, members of the execution court, were found guilty of war crimes in April 1946, and given prison sentences ranging from five to nine years, as opposed to the life sentences imposed on the Americans in 1942.

Capt. Chase Nielsen came back to China to be a principal witness for the prosecution.

Four captured airmen. Lt. Dean Hallmark (top left), Lt. Robert Hite (top right), Lt. Robert Meder (bottom left), and Lt. William Farrow (bottom right). Hallmark and Farrow were executed, Meder died in prison and Hite survived 40 months in prison. USAF

Dear Mother and Dad:

Three United States aviators who crashed in China after Lt. Gen. James H. Doolittle's first Tokyo raid and were later executed wrote farewell letters. The men were Lt. Dean E. Hallmark of Dallas, Texas, Lt. William G. Farrow of Darlington, S. C., and Sgt. Harold A. Spatz of Lebo, Kans. Copies of the letters were found in Jap military files and were released Feb. 27. The Japs never sent them. Excerpts:

℄ *Hallmark:* "Dear Mother and Dad . . . I went on a bombing mission because I was told to and because I am an Army pilot. I knew there would be some danger, but it was war . . . I never dreamed of this outcome . . . They have just told me I am liable for execution. I can hardly believe it . . . Mother, you try to stand up under this, and pray. And Dad, you do the same. And sister, too. I don't know how to end this letter except by sending you all my love."

℄ *Farrow:* "Dearest Mother . . . Don't let this get you down. Just remember that God will make everything right and that I will see you all again in the hereafter . . . We've had some good times together. Life treated us well and we have much to be thankful for. You are all splendid Christians and knowing and loving you has meant much in my life. So for me, and for America, be brave and live a rich, full life, pray to God and do your best . . . I know, Mom, that this is going to hit you hard . . . I am sorry not to have treated you with more love and devotion, for not giving you all I could, and will you please forgive me? . . . I realize now that you are the best mother in the world . . . so let me implore you— be brave and strong."

℄ *Spatz:* "Dear Dad . . . I want you to know that I died fighting for my country like a soldier. My clothes are all I have that I know of any value. I give them to you; and Dad, I want you to know I love you and may God bless you."

This photo of Lt. George Barr and his Japanese captors was taken a few hours after his capture on the morning of April 19.   AFM

This photograph, which appeared in a Japanese magazine, shows Lt. Robert Hite being led out of a plane in Japan after his capture in Japanese occupied China. He would survive 40 months of imprisonment before returning to the United States at the end of the war. This photograph reached London through neutral channels in February 1943 and was radioed to the news media in the United States.   AFM

Members of Lt. Farrow's crew pose with their Japanese captors in China. From left are DeShazer, Spatz, Hite, Farrow and Barr.   AFM

Sgt. Harold Spatz just after his capture, before he had been tortured. He was only 20. From captured Japanese films.   AFM

Three of the Raiders—Hallmark, Farrow and Spatz—were executed at this cemetery near the Kiangwan Prison, Shanghai, on Oct. 15, 1942. They were made to kneel, tied to small crosses and shot. AFM

Exterior view of Kiangwan Prison compound near Shanghai, where the eight prisoners were held. The building at left was the scene of the "trial," where the death sentences were handed down. AFM

The solitary confinement cell block at the Kiangwan Prison in which the four prisoners were kept. AFM

After 40 months as captives of the Japanese, three of the four ex-prisoners arrived at Chungking in late August 1945. From left are DeShazer, Hite and Nielsen. USAF

Mrs. James Doolittle greets three of the released prisoners in September 1945. From left: Hite, DeShazer and Nielsen. Bob Hite

Three members of Hallmark's crew were captured in a Chinese village house by Japanese troops. Nielsen and Meder tried to hide in the rafters. Hallmark hid behind a bench in a corner.

CHAPTER SEVEN

EFFECTS OF THE RAID

TO MIDWAY AND BEYOND

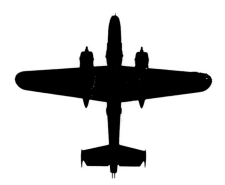

If one were to tally up the pluses and minuses of the raid from a purely military standpoint, the minuses would win hands down. The bombing had a minimal effect on Japan's war production and military capabilities. All 16 B-25s were lost at a time when America needed every plane it could produce. Seventeen aviators, or twenty percent of the aircrew force, were lost for all or part of the war. The deaths of several hundred thousand Chinese civilians and the loss of some Chinese territory can be directly attributed to the raid.

Col. Doolittle at the time considered the raid a failure because of the loss of men and planes.

A great risk was taken in moving a 16-ship, 10,000-man task force so close to the enemy's shores. Especially vulnerable were two aircraft carriers which the United States could ill afford to lose at this critical time in the Pacific war. Had it been worth it?

Many historians say yes. The psychological and strategic plus of the raid, they say, completely overshadowed the minuses on the military side. In simple terms, the Doolittle raid was a turning point of the war. It accomplished several very important things:

- It planted a seed of doubt in the minds of the Japanese people, who until this time had never doubted the impregnability of "Fortress Japan."

- It forced the Japanese to strengthen their home defenses, thus diverting resources that could have been used to expand their military boundaries.

- It gave a morale boost to the American people and their allies at a time when it looked as if there were no way to stop the Japanese from marching across the Pacific. Australia was in jeopardy; Hawaii, Alaska and even the West Coast of the United States seemed vulnerable to attack. America needed an emotional shot in the arm and some genuine heroes to look up to.

- Perhaps most importantly, the raid forced the Japanese to rethink and reanalyze their military strategy in the Pacific. Their Pacific victories had come more quickly than even the Japanese military chiefs had hoped, and uppermost in their minds was the need for a knockout blow to the U.S. Pacific Fleet. Adm. Yamamoto, the architect of the Pearl Harbor attack, had long advocated the capture of Midway Island. By doing so, he reasoned, the American fleet could be drawn to a final battle and finished off. The deadly American carriers, absent when the Japanese attacked Pearl Harbor, were still on the prowl, and had to be destroyed.

Not everyone in the Japanese high command agreed with Yamamoto, but the Doolittle raid convinced everyone that America's carriers had to be destroyed. At first reluctant to commit such a large naval force in the Pacific, Japanese leaders now abandoned all objections to Yamamoto's plan and went ahead with the Midway campaign. Moreover, the military wanted to make up for the embarrassment of having allowed American bombers to violate the Japanese homeland.

Midway Island and certain islands in the Aleutian chain were to be invaded, thereby drawing the U.S. Pacific Fleet into battle. Both thrusts turned into disasters for the Japanese military. The Battle of Midway, a victory for America's air and sea power, blunted any further moves by Japanese forces in that area. The occupation of two islands in the western Aleutians attracted no great fleets, and tied up thousands of Japanese troops and dozens of ships for more than two years to no important strategic purpose.

Although the United St

pine Islands soon after the Doolittle raid and a few islands in the Aleutian chain in June 1942, the Tokyo raid and Battle of Midway a few weeks later together turned the Pacific war around. Many battles lay ahead, but Doolittle's 80 airmen proved that Americans could dish out the same stuff they had been taking from the enemy during the first grim days of the war.

The feeling on the Japanese home front is reflected in a letter the air-ace Saburo Sakai received from his school-girl cousin.

"I know you are in the thick of combat and your successes against the enemy are of great comfort to all of us at home. The bombing of Tokyo and several other cities has brought about tremendous change in the attitude of our people toward the war. Now things are different. Bombs have been dropped here on our homes. It does not seem anymore that there is such a great difference between the battle front and the home front."

Months after the raid, the news media continued to speculate about how the Tokyo raiders had managed to pull it off. A year passed before it was revealed that the planes from "Shangri-La"* had actually taken off from the deck of the *Hornet* (the carrier had been sunk six months after the raid at the Battle of Santa Cruz, on Oct. 27, 1942). More than 10,000 Navy and Air Corps personnel actually knew the story of the raid, but no one revealed the details until they came from official sources in 1943.

National magazines—*Life, Time, Colliers,* and *Reader's Digest*—carried stories and photographs of the event months afterward. In 1943, Lt. Ted Lawson, pilot of Plane #7, wrote his story—*Thirty Seconds Over Tokyo,* the first first-person account. It was serialized in *Colliers* in May 1943 and was made into a movie by Metro Goldwyn Mayer in 1944. A second film, *The Purple Heart,* was produced in the same year. It portrayed the trial of the eight captured Tokyo Raiders. Both films provided a patriotic incentive to the wartime population.

The media in America ensured that the daring deeds of the raiders from "Shangri La" would not be forgotten by the American people.

*A term President Roosevelt had coined when asked where the B-25s had been based when they launched their attack. The term was from James Hilton's novel, *Lost Horizon.*

Rijozo Asano (left) looks through the wreckage of his steel mill after the raid on April 18, 1942. Owner of steel mills in Japan, Korea, China and Manchuria, he was a spokesman for Japanese industrialists, some of whom were opposed to the war. This photo appeared in the Oct. 29, 1945, issue of Life *magazine.*

Courtesy: Time/Life Inc.

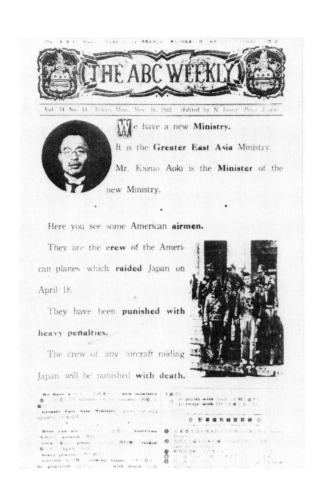

Bomb damage on the Ginza, Tokyo's main thoroughfare after the raid.

The ABC Weekly issue of Nov. 16, 1942, a news sheet printed for Japanese school children, emphasized Japan's victories and denigrated the Allies. The photo shows the captured airmen in China. The news sheet was apparently published in English with a Japanese vocabulary for the study of the English language.

FOR VICTORY BUY UNITED STATES WAR BONDS AND STAMPS

WEATHER
Cooler tonight; frost if sky clears
Temperature at noon, 45.

Columbus Evening Dispatch

OHIO'S GREATEST HOME DAILY

Associated Press News, Wide World Features, Wirephotos International News Service

VOL. 71, NO. 292. *** Telephone—MAin 1234 COLUMBUS, OHIO, SATURDAY, APRIL 18, 1942 16 PAGES PRICE 3 CENTS

U.S. WARPLANES RAIN BOMBS ON LEADING CITIES OF JAP EMPIRE

YANK BOMBING PLANES CARRY WAR TO ENEMY

(By The Associated Press)

AMERICAN bombers lashed at the Axis on far-flung battlefronts today, and military observers estimated that the Allies were throwing nearly 3000 first line warplanes against the enemy every 24 hours.

Informed sources declared the vast new aerial offensive was beginning to wrest the initiative in sector after sector on all war fronts.

With American assembly lines rolling off an endless stream of fighters and bombers, these were today's proofs of their punching power:

1. Planes identified as American bombed Tokyo and other Japanese cities for the first time in history.

2. U. S. army bombers operating from bases in India pounded Japanese-occupied Rangoon, Burma, a key springboard for enemy naval operations in the Bay of Bengal and for the land drive in Burma.

3. American-built Boston (Douglas) planes joined in the RAF's non-stop offensive against the German-occupied French "invasion coast."

4. Allied warplanes, presumably including United States aircraft, again blasted Japanese-held Koepang, in Dutch Timor, where the Japanese have been massing for attacks on Australia.

"America is becoming a deciding factor in the war," a London military expert said, pointing to the widespread raids.

"For the first time, she is actually placing an effective number of planes in distant fighting lines, which means that the battle of production and transportation is being won.

"From now on, it's going to be planes, planes and more planes in India, Egypt, Britain, Australia, China and every other battlefront until the initiative everywhere is ours.

"Japan threw her maximum strength in the initial attacks. Her air position cannot improve. Germany and Italy have shown a steady decline in their air strength since last year."

HUNDREDS OF BUILDINGS REPORTED WRECKED IN RAID ON JAPS

Tokyo was playing air raid when this picture was taken. Smoke from a practice incendiary fire rises from the plaza directly in front of Tokyo's main railway station. Japanese civilians have been trained by such demonstrations for several years in preparation for the real thing that happened Saturday. (AP). Wirephoto.

In another rehearsal for the air raid that finally came members of the women's fire-fighting brigade are pictured in an air-raid drill on the Ginza, Tokyo's Broadway. This drill took place before the war with the U. S.

(OTHER TOKYO PICTURES ON PAGE 2-3)

Japanese reports Saturday revealed that warplanes, identified as American, had raided (1) The Tokyo-Yokohama area and the cities (2) of Nagoya and Kobe. The Berlin radio reported a fire of unannounced origin destroyed more than 400 buildings and killed a number of persons in Oguni (3) The raid caused air raid warnings across 800 miles of the Japanese archipelago. (AP). Wirephoto.

Tokyo, Yokohama, Kobe And Nagoya Hit in Big Three-Hour Offensive

(By the Associated Press)

TOKYO, (From Japanese Broadcasts), APRIL 18.—The Japanese command announced that hostile warplanes bombed Tokyo, Yokohama, Nagoya and Kobe today and caused air-raid alarms to run through three of the four main islands of Japan. Observers said the raiders over Tokyo bore the insignia of the United States air force.

(The Japanese embassy in Buenos Aires, Argentina, issued a communique saying flatly that the attacking planes were American.) The raids began at 12:30 p. m., Tokyo time, and the all clear was not sounded until three hours and 20 minutes later, the communique said.)

These were the first air raids in Japan's experience.

(Thus in one tremendous sweep, the attackers, in what appears to have been the most daring air assault in history, struck at the heart of the Japanese empire; at Tokyo, the capital, population 7,000,000, the world's third city; Nagoya, 1,400,000, center of the aircraft industry; Kobe, 1,200,000, chief port of the empire, shipping point for supplying the Japanese armed forces in the southwest Pacific; Yokohama, 950,000, the port for Tokyo.)

Raid alarms were in force for varying periods from the northern tip of Hokkaido to Shikoku in the south, including most of the main island, Honshu. (This embraces a sweep of more than 1000 miles.)

Imperial headquarters announced that raiders which "approached from several directions" came over the Tokyo - Yokohama area half an hour after noon and that two hours later two planes raided Nagoya and a single raider dropped incendiaries on Kobe. The latter is 376 miles west of Tokyo.

CHUNGKING, APRIL 18.—(AP).—It was learned on most reliable authority tonight that today's air raids on Japan were not based in China. This strengthened belief that an aircraft carrier was used.

Official announcements said that "it is confirmed thus far that nine enemy planes were shot down" in the Tokyo-Yokohama area and that in all cases the damage was light.

(The claim of nine raiders destroyed suggests a raid by a total of many times that number.)

"Observers declared that without doubt the planes which bombed the Tokyo-Yokohama region were United States machines," said the Tokyo radio. "They said the American blue star ensign could be seen clearly from the ground."

Communiques of eastern defense headquarters, in Tokyo, and central defense headquarters, in Osaka, showed that the following regions were under raid alarms for varying periods during the afternoon:

All of Hokkaido, northernmost of the main islands; the Tohoku district, the eastern coast of Honshu above Tokyo; the Tokyo-Yokohama area; the Tokaido, the thickly settled belt along Honshu's southeastern coast between Tokyo and Osaka; the Kyoto-Kobe-Osaka triangle, industrial heart of the empire; the Chugoku district, around Okayama and extending almost to the western tip of Honshu; the island of Shikoku, south of Honshu.

Late in the afternoon it was announced that the western defense headquarters, which includes the fourth of the main

Continued on Page THREE, Column ONE

United Nations On Offensive In Far Pacific

WASHINGTON, APRIL 18.—(AP).—Chairmen of the house military and naval committees maintained today that the bombing of Japanese cities, as described by Tokyo, meant the start of an offensive war by the United Nations in the Far Pacific.

"It is the beginning of a general offensive," asserted Representative May (D) of Kentucky, chairman of the military committee. "While it is hard for me to believe anything Japan says, this bears out my prediction of 10 days ago that Tokyo would be bombed shortly."

Representative Vinson (D) of Georgia, chairman of the naval committee, elated by the report of the aerial attacks, declared that "it appears to me that the Allied nations are beginning to take the offensive."

Although Tokyo said its observers were convinced the raiders were United States warplanes, the army and navy here said they had no confirmation of the reported foray.

Assuming Tokyo to be telling the truth, there are several explanations of the lack of confirmation. If the raiders operated from an aircraft carrier, there would be no reports from the United States forces until their radios could be operated without disclosing ocean positions the enemy would like to know. Thus, the raid of a United States task force on Wake and Marcus islands was not officially announced here for weeks afterwards.

Late War Bulletins

BERLIN, APRIL 18.—(By Official German Wireless)—(INS).—New air raid alarms sounded in various areas of Japan this afternoon, according to the German news agency DNB.

Tokyo had a new alarm at 3 p. m., while the sirens also were sounded in Kyoto, North Osaka and Okayama, 70 miles west of Kobe.

Alerts also were sounded in central Japan from coast to coast.

ROME (FROM ITALIAN BROADCASTS), APRIL 18.—(UP).—An Italian destroyer has sunk a submarine in the central Mediterranean, the Italian high command announced today.

Cebu Falls to Jap Invaders; City Is Reported in Flames

WASHINGTON, APRIL 18. — (INS). — Lieut. Gen. Jonathan M. Wainright reported today that despite continuing fierce resistance by his outnumbered forces, the city of Cebu, second largest in the Philippines, has fallen to the enemy and is reported to be burning.

This was disclosed in a war department communique which also stated that the aerial bombardment and shelling of Corregidor is continuing, but that the defenders have blasted Jap-held roads and bridges on Bataan, disrupting enemy communications.

Fierce resistance also was reported on the important island of Panay, where the Japanese landed recently, apparently in an effort to "cash in" finally on the riches of the Philippines.

$500,000 IN WAR BONDS IS DUE U. S. FLYERS IF TOKYO BOMBING IS CONFIRMED OFFICIALLY

CHICAGO, APRIL 18.—(INS).—Riches—$500,000 or more in war bonds — will be showered upon some American flyer, or group of flyers, if the government officially confirms that American planes have bombed Tokyo.

Ever since Japan's stab-in-the-back on Pearl Harbor, Dec. 7, American Legion posts, clubs and patriotic groups from coast-to-coast have been purchasing war savings bonds and setting them aside for the first American to drop a bomb on Tokyo.

Some of the awards were designated for the first bombing of the Japanese capital by any United Nations flyer. Conservative estimates put the total of the prizes at more than $500,000.

The Rev. Preston Bradley of Chicago is custodian of one $1000 bond purchased by John L. Keeshin, proprietor of a trucking firm, "for the first American flyer to bomb Tokyo—and may he get it soon."

"The bombing of Japanese cities will sacrifice lives, but it also will save millions of lives later in the war," the Rev. Mr. Bradley said. "Force is the only language the Japanese understand."

Authorities on army and navy law disagreed as to whether officers and men could accept the many prizes offered. Should it be interpreted that they cannot, most of them are expected to go to USO and army and navy relief organizations.

NAVY MAY TAKE OVER OPERATION OF AIRPORT

Possibility that the navy will take over operation of Port Columbus, possibly by May 1, was seen Saturday following a conference Friday afternoon between city officials and a navy representative.

Although Mayor Green and Service Director Grover Clements would not comment on the meeting, discussions apparently centered on a lease agreement between the city and the navy which may be offered to council Monday night.

It also was reported that the city is prepared to offer the navy an alternate site for a base near the Greenlawn avenue bridge if the government decides not to take over the municipal airport.

It is doubtful, however, that the river itself would be of value for seaplane operations because of its winding nature and comparative shallow depths.

Two Courses Open

Should the navy decide to lease the municipal airport, two courses of action are open:

1. The field might be designated as a military airport in which case all commercial flying, both airlines and private, would be banned and the control tower would be manned by navy men.

2. The field might be designated a joint military-civilian airport in which case the control tower would remain under the jurisdiction of the civil aeronautics authority while the field itself would be under control of the navy.

At Louisville, where a similar arrangement exists, the CAA is in charge of the control tower

Continued on Page THREE, Column ONE

HIT-SKIP VICTIM

While crossing South High street near Frankfort street, early Saturday, Donald W. Long, age 23, of 103 West Sixth avenue, was struck by an auto and suffered ankle and chest injuries. He was taken to St. Francis hospital. Police said the driver of the car failed to stop after the accident.

Increase in Lend-Lease Aid to Russia Reported

WASHINGTON, APRIL 18.—(AP).—The White House today reported a sharp upsurge of lend-lease aid to Russia, saying that two and a half times as much was sent in March as was sent in February.

TRANSFER OF $2,000,000 TO AID DEFENSE SOUGHT

Governor Would Make Poor Relief Surplus Available to Aid Local Defense Councils.

First steps to set up a state "defense relief fund" from which local defense councils will be allocated funds to carry on civilian defense work will be taken Monday when Governor Bricker will request authority from the Ohio control board to transfer a $2,000,000 surplus from the state poor relief fund to the new fund.

If approved, the money would be allocated to the various local defense councils on the basis of the tax duplicate of the municipality over which they have jurisdiction and would be used only to carry on civilian defense activities.

Franklin county would receive approximately $119,400 under the program.

Resolution asking the transfer of the surplus, consisting of $1,500,000 saved in 1941 and $500,000 which it is estimated will be saved this year, was passed at a meeting of the 16-member state defense council Saturday morning. Governor Bricker heads the Ohio council.

The governor said that such a transfer of funds had been declared legal by the attorney general office. Four of the five control board members must approve before the transfer can be made. Members of the board are the state finance director, the state auditor, the attorney general and the chairmen of the house and senate finance committees.

Light Frost Forecast For Columbus Tonight

With temperatures running about 10 degrees below normal Saturday morning, the forecast warned Columbus residents that cooler weather was in store for Saturday night, with light frost if the sky cleared. There was no frost Friday night, the weather bureau reported.

Friday's maximum temperature was followed by a low of 40 degrees at 6 a. m. Saturday. At noon the mercury stood at 45.

NOTED CONDUCTOR DIES

SAN FRANCISCO, APRIL 18.—(AP).—Alfred Hertz, 69, composer and symphony orchestra conductor, authority on Wagnerian interpretation, died today.

Fire Hits Store At Worthington

Blaze Is Witnessed by Hundreds of Spectators.

While hundreds of spectators watched, firemen from Columbus and Worthington brought under control a blaze in Kroger store in High street at Worthington early Saturday.

The fire started in an electric hot plate and firemen broke out the front showcase windows to fight the blaze. While the loss was not officially estimated, officials said the floor and a large meat case were badly damaged.

A ladder and pump company from Columbus went to the scene to aid the village department in fighting the fire.

CHAPTER EIGHT

AFTERMATH AND LEGACY OF THE RAID

THEY WILL NEVER BE FORGOTTEN

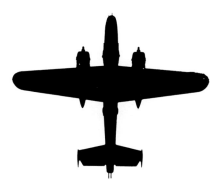

Aftermath

Eventually 64 of the 80 flyers made it to Chungking and safety. Eight remained in China as prisoners of the Japanese, three were killed bailing out or ditching and five were interned in Russia. Early in May 1942 Madame Chiang Kai-Shek presented medals to Doolittle and some of his men.

Many crewmen remained in China or flew on to India for duty in the China-Burma-India theater of war.

Promoted to brigadier general, Doolittle was ordered back to the United States. Upon his arrival at Washington, D.C., he was summoned with his wife, Joe, to the office of President Roosevelt and informed that he was to be the recipient of the nation's highest military medal—the Congressional Medal of Honor.

In September 1942, the new brigadier general was ordered to North Africa to assume command of the Twelfth Air Force.

At Bolling Field near Washington, D.C. on June 27, 1942, Gen. Hap Arnold awarded the Distinguished Flying Cross to 20 officers and three enlisted men who had returned to the United States.

The Doolittle aviators were the toast of the country. They appeared at massive War Bond rallies from one coast to the other. Several Raiders, however, spent these months recovering from injuries. Ted Lawson, who had lost a leg, was seriously injured, as was Charles McClure, who had suffered a fractured shoulder, and Harold Watson who had a dislocated arm. Distinguished Flying Crosses were awarded to these men at Walter Reed Hospital in Washington, D.C.

Lt. Gen. Henry Arnold pinning a medal on Capt. Travis Hoover, while Lt. William M. Bower waits his turn. Gen. Doolittle looks on. The Raider on the extreme right is 2nd Lt. Tom Griffin. USAF (#21282)

On June 27, 1942, Lt. Gen. Henry Arnold presented the Distinguished Flying Cross to 23 of the Tokyo Raiders at Bolling Field, Washington, D.C. USAF (#21281)

In the first such ceremony conducted at Walter Reed Hospital in Washington during the war, Maj. Gen. Millard F. Harmon, chief of staff of the Air Force, pins the Distinguished Flying Cross on 1st Lt. Harold F. Watson. To Harmon's left is 1st Lt. Charles L. McClure; to his right, 1st Lt. Ted W. Lawson. Gen. Doolittle looks on. In the background are Secretary of the Treasury, Henry Morganthau (second from left) and parents and wives of the raiders. Two additional raiders, 2nd Lt. Howard A. Sessler (far right) and 1st Lt. James N. Parker, Jr. (second from right), were also present.   USAF

Capt. Sotojiro Tatsuta, one of seven Japanese officers and men charged with the execution of three raiders, bows to Capt. Chase Nielsen, who was required to bow in the same fashion during his three and one-half years imprisonment. Nielsen returned to China in 1946 to testify at Tatsuta's war-crimes trial. The Japanese officer was sentenced to five years at hard labor; all but nine months of the sentence were served. He died in 1962.   AFM

After returning from China, Lt. Harry McCool, navigator of Plane #4, went on a War Bond selling tour. This photo was taken at the Will Rogers Airport in Oklahoma City in September 1942.
          Harry McCool

SERGEANT DESCRIBES RAID ON JAPAN

Aircraft Plant at Kobe Bombed With 20-Cent Homemade Sight

(Sgt. Edward J. Saylor is only 23, but he has seen what few men alive have seen. He's looked down on Japan at war, and when he finished looking there was a little less of Japan down there to make war. Saylor was one of General Doolittle's men on *that* raid, and we don't have to tell you what raid.

(About Sgt. Saylor, he's a native of Brussett, Montana. He calls it just a little "cross-roads postoffice", but after a few more raids on Japan like the one he went on, he may be able to describe Tokyo in the same manner.

(Saylor finished high school at Jordan, Montana, in 1937 and spent the next two years working in western states as a logger, farm hand and cow puncher. He enlisted in the air corps in 1939. Eglin Field, Florida, was his last American base before he was engaged in active duty over Japan.)

By Sgt. Edward J. Saylor
Engineer-Gunner,
U. S. Army Air Force

OVER KOBE, JAPAN (Delayed) —Hirohito, the Yanks are coming pal!

They're coming with a rush and a roar and some hell to be splattered over this little island empire.

I can hardly wait, bub. We're over Japan now.

It's 1:40 p.m., and a clear day. Below me the country is rugged, but through the valleys the land is streaked with green, with trees and terraces.

Maybe I got a little bit of a catch in my throat, but I don't notice it much. We're just fifteen minutes away from our target, and we're sailing along at four thousand feet. We're flying B-25's, and they're very new and fast.

The skies are empty and clear. We've left the other planes in our squadron, and here we are all alone sitting over several million Japs.

Yes, I have got a catch in my throat, because thinking of all those Japs down there somehow makes me think of Bataan peninsula, and to think of Bataan peninsula makes me sore.

That gives you a strange feeling to be sore when the ground below looks so peaceful and when you see the farmland down below and it looks so damned impersonal.

I used to live out west, and I've never been to Japan before, thank God, but I've heard stories about how they plant stuff on these terraced hillsides in the Far East, and I keep wondering how they work it, having been a farmer once myself.

I am also keeping a sharp watch out for cherry trees. I have been meaning to go to Washington for years to see them, but I have never seen them and I understand they are out of fashion right now.

These are just random thoughts, and all these thoughts probably come and go in a fraction of a second, because I am looking for enemy planes eight to the dozen every second, and there are no more enemy planes than there are cherry trees.

The skies are empty.

I have been sitting here just feeling the throb and roar of the big

B-25. They're beautiful ships, wonderful ships. I think of the other boys off over Tokyo and Yokohama, Osaka and Nagoya now. We're headed for Kobe, to hit the big wharves there, and then over to an aircraft factory where they make Yakashimas. I promise I will get a few of those babies which I understand are being used to strafe our troops. After I pour some lead into those babies, those planes will look like St. Valentine's Day in Chicago has come to the aircraft industry of Japan.

The skies are still empty and vacant, and very clear. It's 1:43 now, and we're all at battle stations.

Our pilot is Lt. Donald G. Smith of San Antonio, Texas, and he knows his business. He can throw this little old ship around like I once saw a guy throw an old Jenny around at a fair back in Montana, and he could do more things with that Jenny than a monkey can do with a coconut. Smith is sure good, all right. When we started coming into Japan, he skimmed the waves so close I could almost taste the salt water from the spray in my mouth, no kidding.

Our navigator-bomber is a guy named Lieut. Howard A. Sessler. He's from Boston, and he's ready to go to work with his bombsight.

Hirohito, you better watch out

THEY WERE OVER TOKYO. *Two men from the ranks who flew with General Doolittle on his bombing raid of Tokyo are shown tracing their flight with the General. On the left is M Sgt. Elred Scott, 34, of Phoenix, Ariz. (promoted since picture was taken) and Sgt. David Thatcher, 20, of Billings, Mont. Each was awarded the Distinguished Flying Cross.*

for guys named Sessler and guys from Boston.

Now this will give you birds a laugh. Here we are sitting up over Japan in a few hundred-thousand-bucks-worth of airplanes, and what kind of bombsight you think we got?

The damned thing cost twenty cents, no kidding. Doolittle—*General Doolittle*—he was afraid that in case any one of us got shot down, we didn't want the Japs to get hold of those Norden bombsights. So we rigged up a sight that cost twenty cents.

But, brother, that sight is going to cost Emperor Hirohito and what they call the Elder Statesmen several million bucks' worth of stuff in a few minutes.

Few minutes! Right now, I mean. We just sighted the outskirts of Kobe. The skies are still vacant, and that scares you a little. 1:52 and we're over the edge of the city.

We're coming in at 2,000 feet. Lieut. Sessler is talking over the interphone in his Boston accent which always gives me a hell of a boot, it sounds so English:

"That's our baby," the looie is saying. "I see the target."

We roar across the city, raising such an almighty racket the noise kind of bounces back, it seems like, and the Japs down there are running back and forth in the streets like so many ants in an ant hill. Buses are running back and forth, but the Japs don't seem to catch on to the fact that the Stars-and-Stripes Forever are right up there over their heads, equipped with plenty of horsepower and plenty of bombs and that darned old 20-

cent bomb sight.

There's our target.

She's an aircraft factory, a mess of buildings down there, scatttered over a block or better. There are the docks.

All we got to do now is let go. Hirohito, the Yanks are coming, sprinkling it along the course.

"Let 'er go, Sess," Smith yells to the bombardier.

I felt her go when she went. The bombs, I mean. Sweet as you please, that B-25 takes a sudden uplift, a little bit of a lurch, and the minute I feel it I know:

Hirohito, the Yanks have arrived.

I can't see where the bombs land, but I know that we're square on the target with the whole works. We're rolling along at 240 m.p.h., now and that ain't any cadence-count either. We're well away from that factory before the hell starts breaking loose and the fires start.

The Japs are waking up, though. They start a mild epidemic—that's what the lieutenant called it—a mild epidemic of anti-aircraft fire.

The stuff comes up like powder-puffs, but we're high-tailing it away from the barrage. The Japs can't estimate our speed, and they never catch up with us. We don't give them a chance, either. We drop right down almost to water level and haul out of there in a hurry, and there I get salt spray, it seems like, in my mouth again.

I wish I could have stuck around to see the look on Hirohito's face when they brought him the messages that night.

D.F.C. for All in Raiding Crews

WASHINGTON. — While Brigadier General Jimmy Doolittle watched with a proud grin, the 20 officers and three enlisted men who helped him bomb Tokyo and other Japanese cities on April 18 received their share of honor here at Bolling Field.

They lined up at attention before a row of bombing planes and Lt. General Hap Arnold, chief of the Air Corps, pinned the Distinguished Flying Cross on each one of their khaki tunics.

The following press release by the War Department (parts have been deleted) was given to the news media on May 19, 1942.

WAR DEPARTMENT
Bureau of Public Relations
PRESS BRANCH
Tel. - RE 6700
Brs. 3425 and 3438

May 19, 1942

IMMEDIATE *RELEASE*

CONGRESSIONAL MEDAL OF HONOR AWARDED TO LEADER OF TOKYO RAID

The War Department today announced that the President has awarded, in the name of Congress, the Medal of Honor to Brigadier General James H. Doolittle, Air Corps, for "conspicuous leadership above and beyond the call of duty, involving personal valor and intrepidity at an extreme hazard to life. With the apparent certainty of being forced to land in enemy territory or to perish at sea, General Doolittle personally led a squadron of Army bombers, manned by volunteer crews, in a highly destructive raid on the Japanese mainland." General Doolittle organized as well as led the air raid on Japan April 18th. The presentation of the Medal was made by the President in person at the White House at 1:00 P.M. today. Mrs. Doolittle was flown to Washington from Los Angeles to welcome her husband home and to be present at his decoration by the President.

The raid was carried out with United States Army medium bombers. It occurred in broad daylight, with the bombers flying at very low altitudes. Only military objectives, including military, naval and industrial facilities, were attacked. The targets were easily discernible and accurately bombed with incendiary and highly-explosive missiles. Wide-spread damage resulted. Some of the fires which were started continued to burn for two days.

Following the raid, General Doolittle was promoted from Lieutenant Colonel to his present rank. He has returned to Washington to make a personal report on the results of the raid.

General Doolittle has been on active duty with the Army since July 1, 1940. During most of that time he has been on procurement duty. For a short time last August he was on duty in England as a member of a special aviation mission headed by Lieutenant General George H. Brett.

END

WAR DEPARTMENT
HEADQUARTERS OF THE ARMY AIR FORCES
WASHINGTON

April 21, 19...

TO ALL PERSONNEL OF THE ARMY AIR FORCES:

In violation of every rule of military procedure and of every concept of human decency, the Japanese have executed several of your brave comrades who took part in the first Tokyo raid. These men died as heroes. We must not rest - we must re-double our efforts - until the inhuman warlords who committed this crime have been utterly destroyed.

Remember those comrades when you get a Zero in your sights - have their sacrifice before you when you line up your bombsights on a Japanese base.

You have demonstrated that the Japanese cannot match you in aerial combat or in bombardment. Let your answer to their treatment of your comrades be the destruction of the Japanese Air Force, their lines of communication, and the production centers which offer them opportunity to continue such atrocities.

H. H. ARNOLD,
General, U. S. Army,
Commanding General, Army Air Forces.

Gen. Arnold sent this message to all Army Air Force personnel upon learning of the execution of three captured Tokyo Raiders. AFM

Next page: The June 1, 1942 issue of Life *magazine devoted two pages to the Doolittle raid. It was not revealed that the bombers were carrier-based. The photos of Davenport, Blanton and Miller are apparently of other flyers.* Author's Collection

U. S. AWARDS MEDALS TO 80 HEROES OF THE ARMY'S BOMBING RAID ON JAPAN

Here are the faces of Americans who bombed Japan. Opposite you see their leader, Brigadier General James H. Doolittle, who on the morning of April 18 swooped astonishingly down out of the Far Eastern skies at the head of his volunteer squadron and spread destruction along a 40-mile swathe in the very heart of the remote island empire. Where these fliers came from and how they returned from their perilous mission are secrets known to few in the U. S. High Command. But

on May 19, at an unexpected ceremony in the White House, President Roosevelt personally bestowed the Congressional Medal of Honor on General Doolittle and let it be known that Distinguished Service Crosses would be awarded to the 79 airmen who soared with him on his brilliant flight.

With Air Chieftain Arnold and Mrs. Doolittle looking on, the President pinned the emblem of the nation's highest honor on General Doolittle's blouse. An accom-

panying citation emphasized that he had undertaken his task "with the apparent certainty of being forced to land in enemy territory or to perish at sea." But not one of his fast B-25 bombers was shot down or prevented from reaching its destination. "We flew low enough," the flier told newspapermen, "so that we could see the expressions on the faces of the people." "And what was that expression?" he was asked. Replied Hero Doolittle: "It was one, I should say, of intense surprise."

MAJOR J. A. HILGER — CAPT. CHARLES R. GREENING — CAPT. DAVID M. JONES — CAPT. E. J. YORK — LIEUT. R. E. MILLER

LIEUT. RICHARD E. COLE — LIEUT. RICHARD KNOBLOCH — LIEUT. TED W. LAWSON — LIEUT. TRAVIS HOOVER — LIEUT. HAROLD F. WATSON

LIEUT. RICHARD O. JOYCE — LIEUT. EVERETT HOLSTROM — LIEUT. JACK A. SIMS — LIEUT. WILLIAM M. BOWER — LIEUT. J. ROYDEN STORK

LIEUT. ROBERT M. GRAY — LIEUT. WILLIAM G. FARROW — LIEUT. DONALD G. SMITH — LIEUT. DEAN DAVENPORT — LIEUT. THADD H. BLANTON

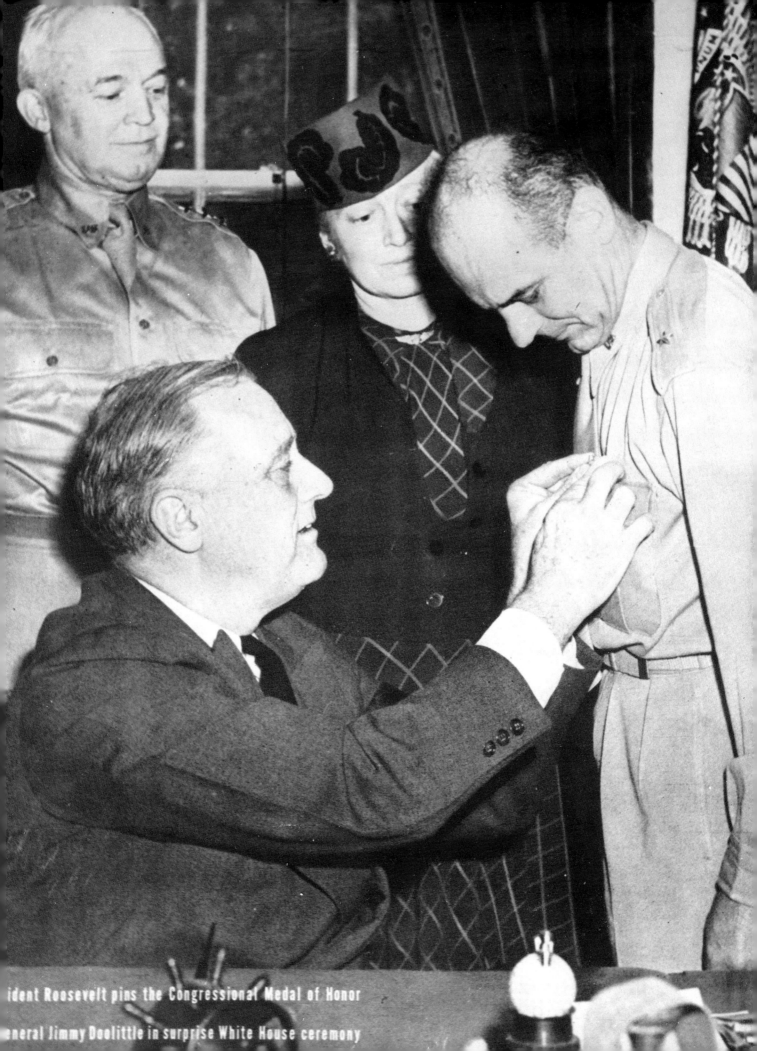

ident Roosevelt pins the Congressional Medal of Honor

eneral Jimmy Doolittle in surprise White House ceremony

Legacy of the Raid

As has been mentioned before, the Tokyo raid could be considered one of the turning points of the war. In the next three and one-half years there would be many more heroic deeds that will forever be etched in the annals of American history. The end of the story was not to take place until August 1945 when the four surviving captured fliers were rescued from their Chinese prison. Actually the end did not come until 1946 when their Japanese captors were put on trial, convicted and imprisoned.

Well over half of the 80 raiders survived the war, an amazing story in itself, considering that the men were in a high-risk wartime occupation—combat flying—and that they were to experience another three and one-half years of war. Besides the seven who lost their lives in the aftermath of the Tokyo raid, 12 more raiders were killed later in the war. After 40 years, 49 raiders survive; they belong to an exclusive club—The Doolittle Toyko Raiders Association, formed in 1963 as a non-profit corporation to further the ideas of the organization and to administer a scholarship fund.

A year to the day after the raid, Doolittle met with a group of the Toyko raiders at a farmhouse in North Africa. They were still fighting a war, though their immediate enemy now was Germany. But they took time to toast their accomplishment and their missing comrades. The general had promised in Chungking to throw a party for all his ''boys,'' but wartime demands scattered the airmen to other theaters of war. This was the best he could do.

It was not until the fall of 1945 that he could get more of the group together. A reunion at the Mac-Fadden Deauville Hotel in Miami cost the general $2,000 out of his own pocket, but the organization was begun. The men decided to meet each year on the anniversary of the raid.

Cups are raised at an informal reunion in a farmhouse in North Africa on April 18, 1943. Attending were Doolittle, some of the raiders and a few crew members who were aboard the Hornet *but did not participate in the actual raid. Doolittle was commander of the 15th Air Force at the time.*

Rockwell International

Every year since, except 1946 and 1951, the Tokyo raiders have met somewhere for several days of comradeship.

In 1958, North American Aviation presented a restored B-25 to the group. It was flown to the Air Force Museum near Dayton, Ohio, for permanent exhibit.

The raiders do not meet annually just for fun or nostalgia, but to honor Air Force units that have conducted good safety records and to award a scholarship to a top senior science or engineering student who plans an aerospace career. The scholarship was established in the name of General Doolittle.

In 1959, the City of Tucson, Ariz., presented the group with a beautiful display case holding 80 silver goblets, one for each of the participants in the raid. The goblets are on display in Arnold Hall of the U.S. Air Force Academy in Colorado Springs. When a raider dies his goblet is inverted. When only two men remain, they will toast each other and their comrades with a special bottle of cognac.

A few of the Raiders returned to civilian life immediately after the war, but 39 of them stayed in the service for a least a few years. The 49 survivors (as of 1983) are now scattered throughout the United States. Most are retired. Col. James H. Macia, Jr., a navigator-bombardier with Plane #14, was the last raider to retire from active military service. He stepped down as chief of staff, Air Force Security Service, at Kelly AFB, Texas, on Oct. 1, 1973.

There are major displays of the Tokyo raid at the Air Force Museum and the National Air and Space Museum, Washington, D.C. A memorial to the raiders has been erected in Valparaiso, Florida, close to Eglin Air Force Base. Gray Air Force Base in Texas and Faktor Dormitory at Chanute Air Force Base, Illinois, were named in honor of two of the Raiders.

The first reunion was held at the MacFadden Deauville Hotel in Miami, Florida, in the fall of 1945. Gen. Doolittle organized the event and paid $2000 of his own money to put it on.
William Bower

Raiders from left: Lt. Richard Cole, Lt. Jack Sims, Lt. Richard Knobloch, Lt. William Fitzhugh, Lt. Everett Holstrom, Lt. Thadd Blanton, Lt. Col. James Doolittle, Sgt. Waldo Bither, Capt. Ross Greening, Lt. Roy Stork, Lt. Richard Joyce, Sgt. Fred Braemer, Sgt. Aden Jones. In the background is Lt. Clayton Campbell, Capt. David Jones, Sgt. Robert Bourgeois, Lt. Frank Kappeler, 2nd Lt. Carl Wildner, Sgt. Joe Manske, Sgt. Jacob Eierman and Sgt. Doug Radney.
Everett Holstrom

The Doolittle Raiders meet on April 18, 1947, at Miami Beach, five years after the historic raid. Reunions have been held every year since 1945, except 1946 and 1951.　　　　USAF (#62856)

Gen. Doolittle receives a plaque containing a fragment of the B-25 ''Whirling Dervish.'' Alexander Burton, right, of North American Aircraft Co. made the presentation at the 1947 Miami Beach reunion.　　　　USAF (#62855)

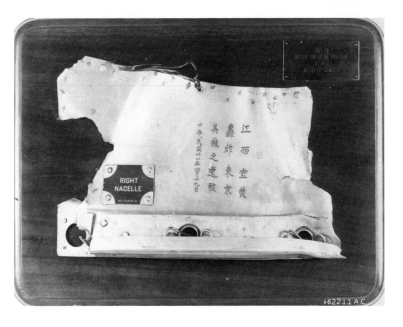

Close-up of the plaque presented to Gen. Doolittle. The fragment of the ''Whirling Dervish,'' which crashed in China, was identified as part of the right engine nacelle. It was recovered by the Rev. Charles L. Mesus, a missionary, who presented it to Bishop Paul Yu Pin, Vicar Apostolic of Nanking. Bishop Yu Pin presented it to Mrs. Franklin D. Roosevelt, who sent it to the Treasury Department for use in war bond sales. After being given to North American Aircraft Co. by the War Finance Division, the fragment was presented to Doolittle's group.

USAF (#62211)

The 1950 reunion was held at the Jackie Cochran-Floyd Odlum Ranch in Palm Springs, California. From left bottom row: Jack Sims, Richard Joyce, Horace Crouch, Thadd Blanton, Charles Mc-Clure, Dean Davenport, Gen. Doolittle, Jacob Manch, Carl Wilder, Ross Greening and William Fitzhugh. Second row: Ed Horton, Jacob Eierman, Ross Wilder, William Pound, Hank Potter, Richard Cole, Howard Sessler, William Bower, Edgar McElroy, Waldo Bither, Robert Bourgeois, Doug Radney, David Pohl. Back row: Aden Jones, Robert Hite, Everett Holstrom, David Jones and Eldred Scott.   William Bower

The traditional "toast" to departed Tokyo Raiders, made at the 1964 reunion in the Western Hills Hotel, Fort Worth, Texas. From left: Richard Knobloch, Everett Holstrom, Robert Emmens, Gen. Doolittle, Charles McClure and Waldo Bither.
Everett Holstrom

Raiders pose on board the USS Yorktown *at the 1979 reunion at Charleston, South Carolina.*
Gen. Knobloch

The Doolittle Tokyo Raiders display at the Air Force Museum at Wright-Patterson AFB, Dayton, Ohio. Various photographs and memorabilia of the participants are vividly displayed to tell the story of the mission. The parachute overhead was used by Lt. Jack Sims when he bailed out over China. AFM

Tung-Sheng Liu, a Chinese interpreter who was instrumental in helping some of the Raiders escape the Japanese, cuts the ribbon at dedication ceremonies for the Tokyo raid display at the Air Force Museum in November 1975. AFM

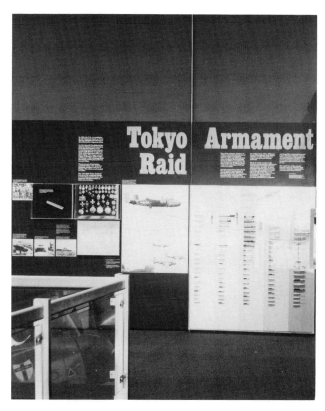

This beautiful tapestry on display at the Air Force Museum was presented to Gen. Doolittle by the Central Bank of Hen-Young, China, shortly after the raid. The inscription alludes to the worldwide fame of the general and his flyers, and congratulates them for their success in bombing the land of the enemy. AFM

Tokyo Raid display at the National Air and Space Museum, Washington, D.C. NASM

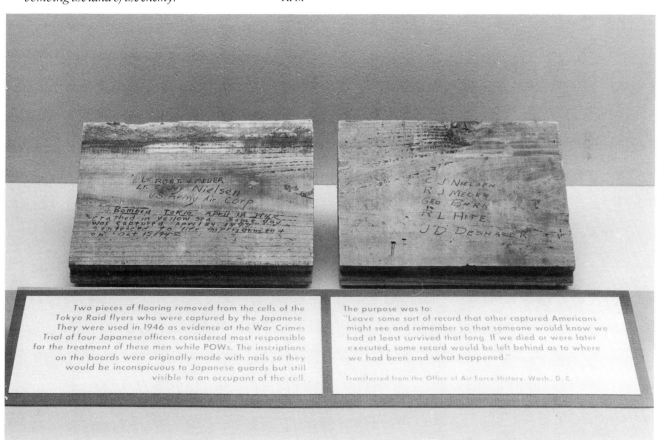

Two pieces of flooring removed from the cells of the Tokyo Raid flyers who were captured by the Japanese. They were used in 1946 as evidence at the War Crimes Trial of four Japanese officers considered most responsible for the treatment of these men while POWs. The inscriptions on the boards were originally made with nails so they would be inconspicuous to Japanese guards but still visible to an occupant of the cell.

The purpose was to:
"Leave some sort of record that other captured Americans might see and remember so that someone would know we had at least survived that long. If we died or were later executed, some record would be left behind as to where we had been and what happened."

Transferred from the Office of Air Force History, Wash., D. C.

This pot was presented to Jimmy Doolittle in Calcutta, India, at the Great Eastern Hotel in May 1942.   William Bower

Gen. Doolittle is shown signing Tokyo raid books in Washington, D.C. on April 14, 1982. Four B-25s made a commemorative flight over the Capitol to honor the 40th anniversary of the Tokyo raid.   Jeff Ethell

Four Raiders meet on May 20, 1978, at the dedication of a dormitory building at Chanute AFB named for Cpl. Faktor, killed in China after bailing out of his plane. From left are Maj. Griffin, Capt. Ozuk, and Gens. Doolittle and Knobloch.   Thomas Griffin

A memorial to the Tokyo Raiders has been placed on the John C. Sims Parkway in Valparaiso, Florida close to Eglin Air Force Base, training site for the air crews in 1942. Niceville-Valparaiso Chamber of Commerce

The Doolittle Raiders silver goblets, on display at the U.S. Air Force Academy, Colorado Springs. Each of the 80 goblets is inscribed with the name of a Raider. When a crew member dies, his goblet is inverted. The last two men will open a special bottle of cognac (vintage 1896, the year of Doolittle's birth) and toast their departed comrades. U.S. Air Force Academy

The Restored B-25B

A B-25B Mitchell, painstakingly converted from a later model, was waiting for General Doolittle and other members of the Tokyo Raiders Association when they gathered for their 12th reunion at Las Vegas in April 1958. The plane was rebuilt from a rare B-25D by North American Aviation, Inc. (now a division of Rockwell International) of Inglewood, Calif., the original contractor.

Doolittle was to fly the plane from Las Vegas to Patterson Field near Dayton, Ohio, where he would present it to the Air Force Museum for permanent display. But severe storms forced him to land at Scott Air Force Base at Bellerville, Ill., on April 21. His Tokyo raid co-pilot, Lt. Col. Richard E. Cole, finished the flight the next day. The General left Scott in a T-33 jet trainer for Washington, D.C., making a brief stop at the museum en route.

For years the plane was displayed outdoors. Then, after some futher restoration work, it was moved to its present location inside the museum.

The B-25B at the Air Force Museum.   AFM

Jimmy Doolittle in the cockpit of the B-25 at Las Vegas.   Rockwell International

Thirty Seconds Over Tokyo and The Purple Heart

Two movies about the Doolittle raiders were produced in 1944.

The best-known was *Thirty Seconds Over Tokyo*, adapted from the book written by Ted Lawson, pilot of the "Ruptured Duck," and edited by Robert Considine. Produced by Sam Zimbalist and directed by Mervyn LeRoy, the MGM film starred Van Johnson as Lawson. Other notable performers included Robert Walker, Spencer Tracy, Robert Mitchum, Leon Ames and Phyllis Thaxter.

To make the movie as realistic as possible given wartime restrictions, the studio shot many scenes on location—at Eglin Field, where the raiders had actually trained, and at Alameda Naval Air Station. The low-level flights were filmed over the Gulf of Mexico and the West Coast. The Port of Oakland served as the Japanese coast, Santa Barbara substituted for the coast of China, downtown Los Angeles doubled for Tokyo and flooded rice fields near Sacramento were used in the China scenes. Bombers of the 952nd B-25 Transition Group at Mather Air Base near Sacramento were used in the flying sequences. They were early-model B-25Cs and Ds.

Ted Lawson was technical director for part of the film; Dean Davenport, Lawson's co-pilot, appeared in some of the flying scenes and took over as technical director when Lawson was recalled to duty.

Directed by Darryl F. Zanuck, *The Purple Heart* was a 20th Century-Fox production starring Dana Andrews, Richard Conte, Farley Granger, Donald Barry and Sam Levene.

The film was based on the Japanese trial and execution of American airmen captured after the Doolittle raid. Piecing together the few details available, the filmmakers produced a dramatic wartime tale noted for its strong patriotic appeal.

Purely fictional was *Destination Tokyo*, a third movie linked to the Doolittle raid. Released on June 1, 1944, the Warner Brothers film starred Cary Grant, John Garfield and Alan Hale. The story centered on a submarine that landed Americans on the shores of Tokyo Bay to report on weather conditions to the *Hornet*, which was steaming toward Tokyo with its B-25s on board. (Though American subs did penetrate Japanese waters at the time of the raid, no Americans were put ashore.)

As recently as the early 1980s, Hollywood was recalling the Tokyo Raiders. "Salvage I," a TV series starring Andy Griffith, included a story about the discovery and salvage of a Doolittle bomber that had crash landed in a remote part of China following the raid.

Lt. Ted Lawson in 1942.   Jim Osborne

Raider Dean Davenport, Ted Lawson's co-pilot on the raid, briefs actor Robert Walker on the B-25 during the filming of 30 Seconds Over Tokyo at Eglin Field, Fla., in early 1944. Davenport served as the film's technical adviser after Lawson was called back to active duty.

James Farmer Collection

The "Ruptured Duck" as it appeared in the movie.

Jim Osborne

"THIRTY SECONDS OVER TOKYO"
PROGRAM NOTES

Spencer Tracy played Lieut. Colonel (now Lieut. General) James H. Doolittle in "Thirty Seconds Over Tokyo" at his own request.

"It is a great honor," Tracy said, "to portray one of America's great heroes."

Tracy was also pleased that every line of dialogue he speaks in the picture was actually spoken by Gen. Doolittle.

Tracy portrays a living man on the screen for the second time in this picture. The first occasion was when he played Father Edward J. Flanagan in "Boys Town." This role won him an Academy award.

☆

"Thirty Seconds Over Tokyo" is said to be the first completely authentic picture that has come out of World War II. There is no fiction in it. Even the names of the characters are the real names of the heroes who made the initial Tokyo bombing mission possible.

Producer Sam Zimbalist read the Ted Lawson story of the raid in galley proofs and urged its purchase for picture purposes. After picture rights had been secured by Metro-Goldwyn Mayer, he worked for months on the preparations for the filming of the story, so that every detail would be absolutely authentic. He even had the biographies of 65 persons connected with the story checked for such details as the color of their eyes, where they had been living for the past few years, to whom they are married, their personal mannerisms and other items. As the result of this careful preparation each of the 65 gave their permission to be represented on the screen.

☆

As Lieut. (now Major) Ted Lawson, Van Johnson has his initial stellar role. When he first read of the Tokyo bombing, he never dreamed he would some day play a leading part in the screen story of the raid. "When I learned Metro-Goldwyn-Mayer had purchased the story I asked Producer Sam Zimbalist to keep me in mind for a role," Johnson recalled. "I meant one of the crew members. No one was more surprised than I was, when given the Ted Lawson role."

☆

Robert Walker, who portrays Corporal (now Staff Sergeant) David Thatcher, set a record for playing G.I. roles on the screen. He made his screen bow over a year ago as a sailor in "Bataan." He was a private in "See Here, Private Hargrove," a corporal in "Since You Went Away," and the only noncommissioned officer in the cast of "Thirty Seconds Over Tokyo." Immediately following completion of the film version of Major Lawson's best-seller, Walker reported for his current role—that of a corporal in "The Clock."

☆

Mervyn LeRoy was one of the first directors to guide eighteen B-25 bombers thousands of feet in the air from a jeep. While filming scenes at an Army Air base in Florida, officers provided LeRoy with a radio-equipped jeep, allowing him to direct the ground cameras, the camera planes, and the bombers, simultaneously.

☆

This picture brings a new and talented leading lady to the screen. She is Phyllis Thaxter, former protege of Lunt and Fontanne in New York, who played the title role in one of the "Claudia" companies on the stage.

☆

During a visit with Producer Sam Zimbalist, Major Ted Lawson revealed that he might never have written his story, except for his wife. He had little ready money when he returned to the United States from China. Ellen Lawson was about to have a baby. Because he wanted her to have the best of care when the baby was born; he agreed to write the story.

☆

Two of the young heroes of the Tokyo raid, who first met on the "Hornet" while enroute to the coast of Japan, celebrated their reunion on the set of "Thirty Seconds Over Tokyo" during its filming. Both were assigned by the Army and Navy to act as technical advisors. Major Dean Davenport, the Ruptured Duck's co-pilot, started a friendship while on the "Hornet" that was renewed for the first time in two years on the set.

☆

To get four huge B-25 bombers onto a set at Metro-Goldwyn-Mayer during the filming of the picture, studio technicians had to bring the ships onto the lot by a back entrance, tear down several small storage buildings, build a 100-foot ramp of heavy timbers, and cut a massive new doorway into the stage.

☆

The cry "print it" after each good take during the filming of "Thirty Seconds Over Tokyo" was abandoned for "ding how." "Ding how" is Chinese for very good.

☆

Five members of the cast hold honorable discharges from the United States Armed Services and the Merchant Marine. Dan DeFore, who plays Lieut. (now Captain) Charles McClure, was in the Air Force. Tim Murdock, who portrays Lieut. (now Major) Dean Davenport, spent a year and a half overseas with the Marine Corps. Jay Norris, Navy destroyer veteran wounded in the South Pacific, appears as Lieut. (now Lieut. Colonel) Rodney "Hoss" Wilder. Gordon McDonald, who portrays the late Lieut. Robert Clever, was in the Merchant Marine.

☆

A company of 93 people, including the cast and Director Melvyn LeRoy, spent more than a month in Florida filming training sequences for the picture. Army and Navy officials cooperated in every way to make the film a true account of a true story. Location site was an Army field in the vicinity of Eglin Field, where the Tokyo raiders trained.

☆

Six-foot, seven-inch Jack Reilly, who plays Lieut. (now first Lieut.) Jacob "Shorty" Manch, used three Army cots for sleeping purposes while on location at Florida. Ordinary cots are just not big enough for the new actor. Reilly, incidentally, is another of those making screen bows in "Thirty Seconds Over Tokyo."

☆

Will Walls, who plays one of the heroic flyers, deserted professional football to portray a role in "Thirty Seconds Over Tokyo." He was the star right end of the New York Giants before turning actor.

☆

Courtesy: Academy of Motion Picture Arts and Sciences.

The following are movie stills from MGM's 1944 movie, Thirty Seconds Over Tokyo, adapted from Capt. Ted Lawson's best-selling book about the Doolittle Raid and the adventures of Lawson's crew in China. The film starred Van Johnson, Robert Walker, Phyllis Thaxter, Robert Mitchum, Leon Ames and Spencer Tracy. Lawson's B-25 was named the "Ruptured Duck." AMPAS

Also in 1944, 20th Century-Fox produced The Purple Heart, *a story of the trial of the eight raiders captured in China. It starred Dana Andrews, Richard Conte, Farley Granger and Sam Levene.*

AMPAS

Donald "Red" Barry and Dana Andrews in a scene from The Purple Heart. *The cockpit scenes were shot in a Lockheed Hudson bomber.* James Farmer Collection

A scene from The Purple Heart. *Actors portraying the captors are, from left: Charles Russell, Richard Conte, Sam Levene, Farley Granger, Dana Andrews, Kevin O'Shea, Donald "Red" Barry and Jim Craven.*
James Farmer Collection

GREENING'S PAINTINGS

The following three paintings depicting incidents of the Doolittle Raid are the work of Capt. Charles Ross Greening, pilot of Plane #11 (the *Hari Carrier*). He served as the raiders' armament officer, and was responsible for the dummy (broom stick) machine guns in the bombers' tail sections and the "Mark Twain" bombsight. After bailing out over China and making it back to the United States, he was reassigned to North Africa. On July 17, 1943, he was shot down over Italy and captured. Two months later he escaped and stayed out of German hands for six months before being cap-

tured again. During his year and-a-half as a POW at Stalag Luft 1, he took up his pre-war interest of painting and produced a remarkable record of his experiences.

After the war he remained in the Air Force, serving as an air attache in Australia and New Zealand. He was only 42 when, in 1957, he died of a rare blood disease. As a tribute to him, his widow, Dorothy, made his paintings available to the Tokyo Raiders and the American Aviation Historical Society. The resulting collection was titled, *Not as Briefed*.

APPENDIX

THE 16 CREWS, PLANE NUMBER, RANK, POSITION IN PLANE, TARGETS, SQUADRON, FATE OF PLANE IN CHINA

Crew No. 1 (Plane #40-2344; target Tokyo)
34th Bombardment Squadron
Pilot: Lt. Col. James H. Doolittle (Air Materiel Command)
Copilot: Lt. Richard E. Cole
Navigator: Lt. Henry A. Potter
Bombardier: S/Sgt. Fred A. Braemer
Flight Engineer/Gunner: S/Sgt. Paul J. Leonard
(Bailed Out)

Crew No. 2 (Plane #40-2292; target Tokyo)
37th Bombardment Squadron
Pilot: Lt. Travis Hoover
Copilot: Lt. William N. Fitzhugh
Navigator: Lt. Carl R. Wildner
Bombardier: Lt. Richard E. Miller
Flight Engineer/Gunner: Sgt. Douglas V. Radney
(Crashed Landed)

Crew No. 3 (Plane #40-2270, "Whiskey Pete"; target Tokyo)
95th Bombardment Squadron
Pilot: Lt. Robert M. Gray
Copilot: Lt. Jacob E. Manch
Navigator: Lt. Charles J. Ozuk, Jr.
Bombardier: Sgt. Aden E. Jones
*Flight Engineer/Gunner: Cpl. Leland D. Faktor
(Bailed Out)

Crew No. 4 (Plane #40-282; target Tokyo)
95th Bombardment Squadron
Pilot: Lt. Everett W. Holstrom
Copilot: Lt. Lucian N. Youngblood
Navigator: Lt. Harry C. McCool
Bombardier: Sgt. Robert J. Stephens
Flight Engineer/Gunner: Cpl. Bert M. Jordan
(Bailed Out)

Crew No. 5 (Plane #40-2283; target Tokyo)
95th Bombardment Squadron
Pilot: Capt. David M. Jones
Copilot: Lt. Ross R. Wilder
Navigator: Lt. Eugene F. McGurl
Bombardier: Lt. Denver V. Truelove
Flight Engineer/Gunner: Sgt. Joseph W. Manske
(Bailed Out)

Crew No. 6 (Plane #40-2298, "The Green Hornet"; target Tokyo)
95th Bombardment Squadron
*Pilot: Lt. Dean E. Hallmark
*Copilot: Lt. Robert J. Meder
 Navigator: Lt. Chase J. Nielsen
*Bombardier: Sgt. William J. Dieter
*Flight Engineer/Gunner: Sgt. Donald E. Fitzmaurice
(Ditched Off Coast)

Crew No. 7 (Plane #40-2261, "The Ruptured Duck"; target Tokyo)
95th Bombardment Squadron
Pilot: Lt. Ted W. Lawson
Copilot: Lt. Dean Davenport
Navigator: Lt. Charles L. McClure
Bombardier: Lt. Robert S. Clever
Flight Engineer/Gunner: Sgt. David J. Thatcher
(Crashed Landed In Water)

Crew No. 8 (Plane #40-2242; target Tokyo)
95th Bombardment Squadron
Pilot: Capt. Edward J. York
Copilot: Lt. Robert G. Emmens
Navigator/Bombardier: Lt. Nolan A. Herndon
Flight Engineer: S/Sgt. Theodore H. Laban
Gunner: Sgt. David W. Pohl
(Landed In Russia)

Crew No. 9 (Plane #40-2303, "The Whirling Dervish"; target Tokyo)
34th Bombardment Squadron
Pilot: Lt. Harold F. Watson
Copilot: Lt. James N. Parker, Jr.
Navigator: Lt. Thomas C. Griffin
Bombardier: Sgt. Wayne M. Bissell
Flight Engineer/Gunner: T/Sgt. Eldred V. Scott
(Bailed Out)

Crew No. 10 (Plane #40-2250; target Tokyo)
89th Reconnaissance Squadron
Pilot: Lt. Richard O. Joyce
Copilot: Lt. J. Royden Stork
Navigator/Bombardier: Lt. Horace E. Crouch
Flight Engineer: Sgt. George E. Larkin, Jr.
Gunner: S/Sgt. Edwin W. Horton, Jr.
(Bailed Out)

Crew No. 11 (Plane #40-2249, "Hari Carrier"; target Yokohama)
34th Bombardment Squadron
Pilot: Capt. C. Ross Greening (89 RS)
Copilot: Lt. Kenneth E. Reddy
Navigator: Lt. Frank A. Kappeler
Bombardier: S/Sgt. William L. Birch
Flight Engineer/Gunner: Sgt. Melvin J. Gardner
(Bailed Out)

Crew No. 12 (Plane #40-2278; target Yokohama)
37th Bombardment Squadron
Pilot: Lt. William M. Bower
Copilot: Lt. Thadd H. Blanton
Navigator: Lt. William R. Pound, Jr.
Bombardier: T/Sgt. Waldo J. Bither
Flight Engineer/Gunner: S/Sgt. Omer A. Duquette
(Bailed Out)

Crew No. 13 (Plane #40-2247; target Yokosuka)
37th Bombardment Squadron
Pilot: Lt. Edgar E. McElroy
Copilot: Lt. Richard A. Knobloch
Navigator: Lt. Clayton J. Campbell
Bombardier: M/Sgt. Robert C. Bourgeois
Flight Engineer/Gunner: Sgt. Adam R. Williams
(Bailed Out)

Crew No. 14 (Plane #40-2297; target Nagoya)
89th Reconnaissance Squadron
Pilot: Maj. John A. Hilger
Copilot: Lt. Jack A. Sims
Navigator/Bombardier: Lt. James H. Macia, Jr.
Flight Engineer: S/Sgt. Jacob Eierman
Gunner: S/Sgt. Edwin V. Bain
(Bailed Out)

*Died as a result of the raid.

Crew No. 15 (Plane #40-2267; target Nagoya)
89th Reconnaissance Squadron
Pilot: Lt. Donald G. Smith
Copilot: Lt. Griffith P. Williams
Navigator/Bombardier: Lt. Howard A. Sessler
Gunner: Lt. Thomas R. White
Flight Engineer: Sgt. Edward J. Saylor
(Crash Landed)

Crew No. 16 (Plane #40-2268, "Bat Out of Hell"; target Nagoya)
34th Bombardment Squadron
*Pilot: Lt. William G. Farrow
Copilot: Lt. Robert L. Hite
Navigator: Lt. George Barr
Bombardier: Cpl. Jacob D. DeShazer
*Flight Engineer/Gunner: Sgt. Harold A. Spatz (Bailed Out)

Reunion Sites:

1945 Miami, Florida	1968 Fort Walton Beach, Florida	1989 Tacoma, Washington
1947 Miami, Florida	1969 Biloxi, Mississippi	1990 San Francisco, California
1948 Minneapolis, Minnesota	1970 Cocoa Beach, Florida	1991 Pensacola, Florida
1949 Miami, Florida	1971 San Antonio, Texas	1992 Columbia, South Carolina
1950 Palm Desert, California	1972 Los Angeles, California	1993 Colorado Springs, Colorado
1952 Galveston, Texas	1973 Houston, Texas	1994 Fresno, California
1953 San Diego, California	1974 Oakland, California	1995 Lexington, Kentucky
1954 Galveston, Texas	1975 Coral Gables, Florida	1996 Sarasota, Florida
1955 Los Angeles, California	1976 Omaha, Nebraska	1997 Las Vegas, Nevada
1956 Tampa, Florida	1977 Memphis, Tennessee	1998 Sarasota, Florida
1957 Fort Walton Beach, Florida	1978 Rapid City, South Dakota	1999 Dayton, Ohio
1958 Las Vegas, Nevada	1979 Charleston, South Carolina	2000 Ogden, Utah
1959 Tucson, Arizona	1980 Newport Beach, California	2001 Fresno, California
1960 Colorado Springs, Colorado	1981 Columbus, Ohio	2002 Columbia, South Carolina
1961 Camden, Arkansas	1982 St. Petersburg, Florida	2003 Travis AFB, California
1962 Santa Monica, California	1983 Carmel, California	2004 Tucson, Arizona
1963 Seattle, Washington	1984 Fort Worth, Texas	2005 Gorton, Connecticut
1964 Fort Worth, Texas	1985 Albuquerque, New Mexico	2006 Dayton, Ohio
1965 Dayton, Ohio	1986 Las Vegas, Nevada	2007 San Antonio, Texas
1967 Oakland, California	1987 Los Angeles, California	2008 Dallas, Texas
	1988 Monterey, California	2009 Columbia, South Carolina
		2010 Dayton, Ohio

The 72 departed participants of the raid (as of April 2010)

Bain, Edwin *S/Sgt.*	Greening, Charles R. *Capt.*	Miller, Richard E. *2nd Lt.*
Barr, George *2nd Lt.*	Hallmark, Dean E. *2nd Lt.*	Nielsen, Chase *2nd Lt.*
Birch, William *S/Sgt.*	Herndon, Nolan *1st Lt.*	Parker, James M. *2nd Lt.*
Bissel, Wayne M. *Sgt.*	Hilger, John A. *Maj.*	Pohl, David W. *Sgt.*
Bither, Waldo J. *Tech Sgt.*	Holstrom, Everett W. *2nd Lt.*	Potter, Henry A. *Lt.*
Blanton, Thadd H. *2nd Lt.*	Hoover, Travis *Lt.*	Pound, William R. Jr. *2nd Lt.*
Bourgeois, Robert C. *M/Sgt.*	Horton, Ed *S/Sgt*	Radney, Douglas V. *Sgt.*
Braemer, Fred A. *S/Sgt.*	Jones, Aden E. *Sgt.*	Reddy, Kenneth E. *2nd Lt.*
Campbell, Clayton J. *Lt.*	Jones, David, *Capt.*	Scott, Eldred V. *Tech Sgt.*
Clever, Robert S. *2nd Lt.*	Jordan, Bert M. *Cpl.*	Sessler, Howard A. *Lt.*
Crouch, Horace E. *2nd Lt.*	Joyce, Richard O. *2nd Lt.*	Sims, Jack *2nd Lt.*
Davenport, Dean *2nd Lt.*	Knobloch, Richard A. *Lt.*	Smith, Donald G. *2nd Lt.*
DeShazer, Jake *Cpl.*	Laban, Theodore H. *S/Sgt.*	Spatz, Harold A. *Sgt.*
Dieter, William J. *Sgt.*	Larkin, George E. Jr. *S/Sgt.*	Stephens, Robert J. *Sgt.*
Doolittle, James H. *Lt. Col.*	Lawson, Ted W. *2nd Lt.*	Stork, J. Royden *Lt.*
Duquette, Omer A. *S/Sgt.*	Leonard, Paul J. *S/Sgt.*	Truelove, Denver V. *2nd Lt.*
Eierman, Jacob *S/Sgt.*	Macia, James H. Jr. *2nd Lt.*	Watson, Harold F. *Lt.*
Emmens, Robert G. *Lt.*	Manch, Jacob E. *2nd Lt.*	White, Dr. Thomas R. *Lt.*
Faktor, Leland D. *Cpl.*	Manske, Joseph W. *Sgt.*	Wilder, Ross R. *2nd Lt.*
Farrow, William G. *2nd Lt.*	McClure, Charles L. *Lt.*	Wildner, Carl R. *2nd Lt.*
Fitzhugh, William N. *2nd Lt.*	McCool, Harry C. *2nd Lt.*	Williams, Adam R. *Sgt.*
Fitzmaurice, Donald E. *Sgt.*	McElroy, Edgar E. *Lt.*	Williams, Griffith P. *Lt.*
Gardner, Melvin J. *Sgt.*	McGurl, Eugene F. *2nd Lt.*	York, Edward J. *Capt.*
Gray, Robert M. *2nd Lt.*	Meder, Robert J. *2nd Lt.*	Youngblood, Lucian N. *2nd Lt.*

BIOGRAPHICAL SKETCHES

Short biographical sketches follow of the 49 survivors (as of 1983) of the Tokyo Raid.

Birch, William L, Staff Sergeant

Born in Calexico, Calif., 1917. Entered Army Air Corps in 1939 and graduated from Bombsight Maintenance School. Bombardier on Plane #11. Received pilot's wings in 1943 and left service in 1945 with rank of second lieutenant. Now lives in Santa Ana, Calif., with wife Barbara.

Bissell, Wayne M., Sergeant

Born in Walker, Minn., 1921. Entered Army Air Corps in 1939 and graduated as bombardier. Bombardier on Plane #9. Received pilot's wings in 1943 and flew B-25s in Pacific. Left service in 1945 with rank of first lieutenant. Now retired and lives in Vancouver, Wash.

Bither, Waldo J., Technical Sergeant

Born in Linnew, Maine, 1906. Graduated from Ricker Classical Institute. Entered Army in 1925 and served in Philippines until 1928. Graduated from Armorer and Bombardier-Navigator School. Bombardier on Plane #12. After raid he served as aircraft maintenance officer in Europe and Japan. Retired as major in 1954 and was subsequently employed by General Services Administration. Retired in 1971 and lives in Aledo, Texas, with wife Sue.

Bourgeois, Robert C., Master Sergeant

Born in Lecompte, La., 1917. Entered Army Air Corps in 1939 and graduated from Bombsight Maintenance School. Bombardier on Plane #13. Remained in CBI Theater until July 1943. Retired from service in 1969 with rank of warrant officer. Now associated with exterminating company and lives in Metairie, La., with wife Thelma.

Bower, William M., Second Lieutenant

Born in Revenna, Ohio, 1917. Entered Army Air Corps in 1939 and received pilot's wings in 1940. Pilot on Plane #12. North Africa, Italy and England for duration of war. Remained in Air Force until retiring as a colonel in 1966. Worked in real estate for many years and is now retired and lives in Boulder, Colo., with wife Lorraine.

Braemer, Fred A., Staff Sergeant

Born in Seattle, Wash., 1917. Entered Army Air Corps in 1935 and attended Military Intelligence, Bombardier and Navigator schools. Bombardier on Plane #1. Remained in CBI Theater until July 1943 and then commissioned a second lieutenant. Left Army in November 1945 and re-enlisted as enlisted man during Korean War. Retired as captain in 1968 and lives in Niangua, Mo., with wife Lucille.

Campbell, Clayton J., Second Lieutenant

Born in St. Maries, Idaho, 1917. Obtained B.S. degree from University of Idaho in 1940. Entered Army Air Corps in 1940 and graduated from Navigator School in 1941. Navigator on Plane #13. Remained in CBI Theater after raid. Separated from service in 1945. Retired as lieutenant colonel in reserves. Now lives in Boise, Idaho, with wife Mary.

Cole, Richard E., Second Lieutenant

Born in Dayton, Ohio, 1915. Entered Army Air Corps in 1940 and received pilot's wings in 1941. Copilot on Plane #1. Remained in CBI Theater until July 1943 and again from October 1943 to June 1944. Remained in service until 1947 and returned to active duty in late 1947. Stationed in Venezuela and United States. Retired a colonel in 1967 and is presently a custom home builder in San Antonio, Texas. He lives there with his wife Martha.

Crouch, Horace Ellis, Second Lieutenant

Born in Columbia, S.C., 1918. Graduated with B.S. degree from The Citadel in 1940. Served in National Guard from 1937 to 1940. Entered Army Air Corps in 1940 and graduated from Bombardier, Navigator and Radar schools. Navigator/Bombardier on Plane #10. Remained in CBI Theater until June 1943. After war was stationed in Pacific, Europe and North Africa; retired as a lieutenant colonel in 1962. Has been school consultant in childhood home Columbia, S.C., where he lives with wife Mary.

Davenport, Dean, Second Lieutenant

Born in Spokane, Wash., 1918. Entered Army Air Corps in 1941 and received pilot's wings in 1941. Copilot on Plane #7. Remained in India until October 1942. Served as technical advisor for movie *Thirty Seconds Over Tokyo*; stationed in Alaska from 1944 to 1947. Flew combat missions during Korean War. Retired as colonel in 1967 and worked for utility company in Panama City, Fla., where he now resides with wife Mary.

DeShazer, Jacob Daniel, Corporal

Born in West Stayton, Ore., 1912. Entered Army Air Corps in 1940 and graduated from Bombardier and Airplane Mechanics schools. Bombardier on Plane #16. Captured by Japanese and spent 40 months as prisoner-of-war. Graduated from Seattle Pacific College in 1948 and went into missionary training. Returned to Japan in 1948 as missionary and spent many years converting his former enemies, including Mitsuo Fuchida, leader of the Japanese air attack on Pearl Harbor. Still involved part-time in religious work in his retirement home in Salem, Ore., where he lives with wife Florence. In July 1982 returned to China to visit sites of his imprisonment.

Doolittle, James H.—See text

Eierman, Jacob, Staff Sergeant

Born in Baltimore, Md., 1913. Entered Army Air Corps in 1935. Flight Engineer on Plane #14. Transferred to Anti-Submarine duty on the U.S. East Coast until February 1945. Commissioned a 2nd Lt. in 1945. Retired in 1957 as a major after duty in Germany and Japan. Now lives in Ft. Walton Beach, Fla.

Emmens, Robert G., Second Lieutenant

Born in Medford, Ore., 1914. Entered Army Air Corps in 1937 and received pilot's wings in 1938. Copilot on

Plane #8. Landed in Russia after raid and was interned for 13 months before escaping into Iran in June 1943. Author of *Guests of the Kremlin*. Retired as colonel in 1965 after assignments in Rumania, Austria, Japan and various bases in the United States. Presently a real estate salesman in Medford, Ore., where he lives with wife Justine.

Griffin, Thomas Carson, Second Lieutenant

Born in Green Bay, Wis., 1916. Graduated from University of Alabama with a B.A. degree in 1939. Entered Army (Coast Artillery) in 1939 and transferred to Air Corps in 1940. Graduated from Navigator School in 1940. Navigator on Plane #9. After raid was transferred to North Africa. Shot down and captured by Germans in 1943 and was prisoner-of-war until end of war. Retired in 1980 from own accounting business. Now lives in Cincinnati, Ohio, with wife Esther.

Herndon, Nolan Anderson, First Lieutenant

Born in Greenville, Texas, 1918. Entered Army Air Corps in 1940 and graduated from Navigator School in 1941. Also completed bombardier training. Navigator/Bombardier on Plane #8. Landed in Russia and interned until escaping in June 1943. Remained in United States until end of war. Left service in 1945 as major and retired in 1983 as salesman. Now lives in Edgefield, S.C., with wife Julia.

Hite, Robert L., Second Lieutenant

Born in Odell, Texas, 1920. Entered Army Air Corps in 1940 and received pilot's wings in 1941. Copilot on Plane #16. Captured by Japanese after raid and held as prisoner-of-war for 40 months. Remained in service until 1947 and recalled to active duty during Korean War. Left service again in 1955 and managed hotels in Arkansas and Tennessee for many years. Now retired and lives in Enid, Olka., with wife Portia.

Holstrom, Everett W. Jr., Second Lieutenant

Born in Cottage Grove, Ore., 1916. Graduated from Oregon State University in 1939. Entered Army Air Corps in 1939 and received pilot's wings in 1940. Sank first Japanese submarine off the West Coast, Dec. 24, 1941. Pilot on Plane #4. Remained in CBI Theater after raid until July 1943. After war was assigned to Strategic Air Command and SHAPE until retirement as a brigadier general in 1969. Now lives in Carmel, Calif., with wife Harriet.

Hoover, Travis, Second Lieutenant

Born in Melrose, N.M., 1917. Entered Army Air Corps in 1939 and received pilot's wings in 1940. Pilot on Plane #2. Remained in CBI Theater after raid until June 1942 when he was transferred to England. Also served in North Africa and Italy. Retired from service after various postwar stateside assignments. Received B.A. degree from the University of California in 1949. Now involved in real estate investments and lives in San Antonio, Texas, with wife Kay.

Horton, Edwin Weston Jr., Staff Sergeant

Born in North Eastham, Mass., 1916. Entered Army in 1935 and Army Air Corps in 1938. Graduated from Gun Turret-Maintenance School, Aircraft Mechanics and Armorer schools. Gunner on Plane #10. Remained in CBI Theater until July 1943. After the war worked for Civil

Service at the old training site at Eglin Air Force Base. Now retired and lives in Fort Walton Beach, Fla., with wife Monta.

Jones, Aden Earl, Sergeant

Born in Flint, Mich., 1920. Entered Army Air Corps in 1939. Bombardier on Plane #3. Remained in CBI Theater until July 1943. Rotated back to the United States for duration of war. Discharged in 1948. Now retired and lives in Pomona, Calif., with wife Doris.

Jones, David M., Captain

Born in Marshfield, Ore., 1913. Graduated from University of Arizona in 1936. Entered Army Air Corps in 1937 and received pilot's wings in 1938. Pilot on Plane #5. After raid was transferred to North Africa where he was shot down on Dec. 4, 1942. He was a prisoner-of-war for the duration of war. After the war held various assignments with the Air Force in the United States and Europe and commander of the Air Force Eastern Test Range in Florida for Manned Space Flights. Retired as a major general on May 31, 1973, and now lives in Indialantic, Fla., with wife Anita.

Jordan, Bert M., Corporal

Born in Covington, Okla., 1919. Entered Army Air Corps in 1939. Flight Engineer/Gunner on Plane #4. Remained in CBI Theater until 1943. Served throughout the world after the war in the Air Force until his retirement as chief master sergeant in 1971. Now lives in Pottsboro, Texas, with wife Judy.

Joyce, Richard Outcalt, Second Lieutenant

Born in Lincoln, Neb., 1919. Entered Army Air Corps in 1940 and received pilot's wings in 1941. Pilot on Plane #10. Remained in CBI Theater until December 1942. Transferred back to the United States and separated from the Service in 1946. Since the war he has been in the hardware business in his hometown of Lincoln, Neb., where he lives with wife Dru.

Kappeler, Frank Albert, Second Lieutenant

Born in San Francisco, Calif., 1914. Received a B.S. degree in Aeronautical Engineering from Polytechnic College of Engineering, Oakland, Calif., in 1936. Entered U.S. Navy in 1936 and transferred to Army Air Corps where he graduated as a navigator in 1941. Navigator on Plane #11. Remained in CBI Theater until August 1942. Reassigned to Europe for remainder of war. Retired from the Air Force in 1966 with rank of lieutenant colonel after various assignments in the United States and Japan. Now owns a real estate business in Santa Rosa, Calif., where he lives with wife Betty.

Knobloch, Richard A., Second Lieutenant

Born in Milwaukee, Wisc., 1918. B.S. degree from Kansas State University. Entered Army Air Corps in 1940 and received pilot's wings in 1941. Copilot on Plane #13. Remained in CBI Theater until 1943. Transferred back to United States for duration of war. After war was attached to Royal Air Force, Air Attache to Italy and various command positions. Retired as a brigadier general in 1970. Worked for United Technologies Corp. and is now retired and lives in San Antonio, Texas, with wife Rosemary. Chairman of Doolittle Toyko Raiders Assoc.

Lawson, Ted W., Second Lieutenant

Born in Fresno, Calif., 1917. Graduated from Los Angeles City College with a degree in Aero Engineering. Entered Army Air Corps in 1940 and received pilot's wings in 1940. Pilot on Plane #7. Lost his leg as a result of the raid. Wrote the book, *Thirty Seconds Over Tokyo*, which was adapted into a movie in 1944. Served in Chile and the U.S. during the war, separated in 1945. Owned his own machine shop and worked for North American Aviation and Reynolds Metal Company. Now retired and lives in Chico, Calif., with wife Ellen.

Macia, James Herbert, Second Lieutenant

Born in Tombstone, Ariz., 1916. Entered Army Air Corps in 1940 and graduated from Navigator School in 1941. Navigator/Bombardier on Plane #14. After raid was transferred to Europe for rest of war. Left service in 1946 and recalled in 1951. Retired in 1973 as a colonel, the last Raider to remain in the service. Now works in Catholic Services in San Antonio, Texas, where he lives with wife Mary Alice.

Manske, Joseph W., Sergeant

Born in Gowanda, N.Y., 1921. Entered Army Air Corps in 1939. Graduated from Aircraft Mechanics School. Flight Engineer/Gunner on Plane #5. After raid was commissioned a second lieutenant and served in Europe. Retired from the Air Force as a colonel in 1973. Lives in San Antonio, Texas with wife Phyllis.

McClure, Charles L., Second Lieutenant

Born in University City, Mo., 1918. Received engineering degree from University of Missouri in 1941. Entered Army Air Corps in 1941 and completed Navigator School. Navigator on Plane #7. Hospitalized as a result of the raid for several periods during the war. Received a medical discharge in April 1945. Spent 30 years with a company in Appleton, Wisc., and is still active in business from his home in Black Creek, Wisc., where he lives with wife Edith.

McCool, Harry C., Second Lieutenant

Born in La Junta, Colo., 1918. Received B.S. degree from Oklahoma Southwestern State College in 1940. Entered Army Air Corps in 1940 and graduated from Navigator School in 1941. Navigator on Plane #4. Remained in CBI Theater until Sep. 1942 then assigned to Europe. Had a varied career with the Air Force in the U.S. and overseas until retirement in 1966 with the rank of Lt. Col. Civil Service duty with the Navy in Hawaii until his second retirement in 1980. Now lives in Pearl City, Hawaii, with wife Laverne.

McElroy, Edgar E., Second Lieutenant

Born in Ennis, Texas, 1912. Entered Army Air Corps in 1940 and received pilot's wings in 1941. Pilot on Plane #13. Remained in the CBI Theater until 1943. Held command positions during the war including service with the 6th Bomb Group flying B-29s from Tinian in the Pacific. Postwar service in Europe and Asia, retiring as a lieutenant colonel in 1962. Now retired after years as a factory representative. Lives in Lubbock, Texas, with wife Agnes.

Nielsen, Chase Jay, Second Lieutenant

Born in Hyrum, Utah, 1917. Entered Army Air Corps in 1939 and graduated from Navigator School in 1940. Navigator on Plane #6. Captured by the Japanese and spent 40 months as a prisoner-of-war. Remained in Air Force with various U.S. and overseas assignments until retirement in 1961 with the rank of lieutenant colonel. Worked in private industry until second retirement in 1981. Presently associated with Dominion Capitol Resources in Salt Lake City, Utah. Lives in Brigham City, Utah, with wife Cleo.

Ozuk, Charles John, Second Lieutenant

Born in Vesta Heights, Pa., 1916. Entered Army Air Corps in 1939 and graduated from Navigator School in 1940. Navigator on Plane #3. Remained in CBI Theater until July 1942. Reassigned to North Africa for remainder of war. Now retired and lives in Mundelein, Ill., with wife Georgian.

Parker, James M. Jr., Second Lieutenant

Born in Houston, Texas, 1920. Entered Army Air Corps in 1940 and received pilot's wings in 1941. Copilot on Plane #9. After raid transferred to North Africa. Served in Europe until separation from Air Force in 1947. Now retired and lives in Houston, Texas, with wife Vonda.

Pohl, David N., Sergeant

Born in Boston, Mass., 1921. Entered Army Air Corps in 1940. Gunner Plane #8. Interned in Russia for 13 months after raid. Received pilot's wings in 1945 and left service in 1947 with rank of first lieutenant. Received B.S. degree from Babson Institute, Boston, Mass., and worked as a marketing analyst until retiring in 1975. Now lives in Manhattan Beach, Calif.

Potter, Henry A., Second Lieutenant

Born in Pierre, S.D., 1918. Entered Army Air Corps in 1940 and graduated Navigator School in 1941. Navigator on Plane #1. Transferred to United States after raid. Retired from Air Force in 1970 as a colonel. Now lives in Austin, Texas, with wife Adell.

Radney, Douglas V., Sergeant

Born in Mineola, Texas, 1917. Entered Army Air Corps in 1936 and completed Aircraft Mechanic's School. Flight Engineer/Gunner on Plane #2. Remained in CBI Theater until Sept. 1942. Received pilot's wings in 1945. Retired in 1959 as a major after duty in Alaska. Corporate pilot from 1959-1970. He is now a minister after graduating from a Bible Training Center in 1980 and lives in Casa Grande, Ariz., with wife Mary Jane.

Saylor, Edward Joseph, Sergeant

Born in Brussett, Mont., 1920. Entered Army Air Corps in 1939 and attended Aircraft Maintenance School. Flight Engineer on Plane #15. Transferred to England after raid accepted commission. Retired in 1967 as a major after 28 years in Air Force. Involved in real estate, home construction and currently in a family-owned restaurant in Graham, Wash., where he lives with wife Lorraine.

Sessler, Howard Albert, Second Lieutenant

Born in Boston, Mass., 1917. Entered Army Air Corps in 1940. Completed bombardier and navigator training. Navigator/Bombardier on Plane #15. Remained in CBI Theater until July 1942. Served for duration of war in Mediterranean area and Europe. Separated from service in 1945 with rank of major. B.S. degree in engineering from UCLA in 1950. President of construction firm and lives in Moorpark, Calif., with wife Anna Bell.

Sims, Jack A., Second Lieutenant

Born in Kalamazoo, Mich., 1919. B.A. degree Western Michigan University, 1940. Entered Army Air Corps in 1940 and received pilot's wings in 1941. Copilot on Plane #14. Remained in India until Aug. 1942. Served in Africa flying B-26s. Served in many Air Force positions in United States and England before retiring as a colonel. Now engaged in real estate in Naples, Fla., where he lives with wife Lee.

Stork, J. Royden, Second Lieutenant

Born in Frost, Minn., 1916. Entered Army Air Corps in 1940 and received pilot's wings in 1941. Copilot on Plane #10. Remained in India until 1943. Returned to United States and flew for Air Transport Command. Left service in Oct. 1945 with rank of captain. Spent 36 years as a make-up artist in Hollywood before retiring in 1982. Now lives in Los Angeles, Calif., with wife Kay.

Thatcher, David J., Sergeant

Born in Bridger, Mont., 1921. Entered Army Air Corps in 1940 and graduated from Airplane and Engine Mechanics School in 1941. Flight Engineer/Gunner on Plane #7. Transferred to North Africa and England until Jan. 1944. Left service in July 1945 with rank of staff sergeant. Worked for U.S. Postal Service until retiring in 1979. Now lives in Missoula, Mont., with wife Dawn.

Watson, Harold F., Second Lieutenant

Born in Buffalo, N.Y., 1916. Entered Army Air Corps in 1940 and received pilot's wings in 1941. Pilot on Plane #9. Injured upon bailing-out and upon return to United States was patient at Walter Reed Hospital until July 1944. Retired as a lieutenant colonel from Air Force in 1961 after duty in the United States and Japan. Now lives in Inglewood, Calif.

White, Thomas Robert, First Lieutenant

Born in Haiku, Hawaii, 1909. B.S. degree California Institute of Technology in 1931. M.D. degree from Harvard in 1937. Post graduate training at John Hopkins and interned at Baltimore and Honolulu. Entered Army Air Corps in 1941 and graduated from School of Aviation Medicine in Dec. 1941. Flight Surgeon/Gunner on Plane

#15. Treated some of the injured airmen including Ted Lawson after the raid. Served remainder of war in North Africa, Sicily, Italy, and England. Left the service as a major and practiced in California and Hawaii until retirement. Now lives in Palm Springs, Calif., with wife Marjorie.

Wildner, Carl R., Second Lieutenant

Born in Holyoke, Mass., 1915. B.S. degree from Massachusetts State College in 1938. Entered Army Air Corps in 1939 and graduated from Navigator School in 1941. Navigator on Plane #2. Remained in India until 1943 and returned to United States until end of war. Left service in 1954 as a Lt. Col. after service in Alaska and Germany. Worked in Civil Service for Marine Corps in Philadelphia, Pa., until retirement in 1975. Now lives in Benton, Pa., with wife Hilda.

Williams, Adam Ray, Sergeant

Born in Gastonia, N.C., 1919. Entered Army in 1938 and transferred to Army Air Corps in 1939. Flight Engineer/Gunner on Plane #13. Remained in CBI Theater until 1943. Left service in 1945 with rank of master sergeant. In trucking business after war until retirement. Now lives in Plymouth, N.C., with wife Mary.

Williams, Griffith Paul, Second Lieutenant

Born in Chicago, Ill., 1920. Entered Army Air Corps in 1940 and received pilot's wings in 1941. Copilot on Plane #15. Remained in CBI Theater until July 1942. Transferred to North Africa and shot down, July 1943. Prisoner-of-war until end of war. Retired in 1952 with rank of major. Now lives in El Cajon, Calif., with wife Barbara.

York, Edward J., Captain

Born in Batavia, N.Y., 1912. Entered Army in 1930. Graduated from West Point. Received pilot's wings in 1939. Pilot on Plane #8. Interned in Russia for 13 months. Flew B-17s from Italy. After war was Air Attache in Poland and held many other staff assignments in the Air Force until retirement in 1966 with rank of colonel. Obtained a degree in City Management from University of Texas and was City Manager of Alamo Heights, Texas. Now retired and lives in San Antonio, Texas, with wife Mary Elizabeth.

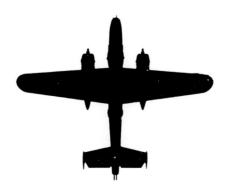

Joe Manske

Richard Knobloch

Dick Cole

Chase Nielsen

Jake DeShazer

Dave Jones

Horace Crouch

Edgar McElroy

Dave Thatcher

Frank Kappeler

Robert Emmens

Nolan Herndon

Bill Bower

Royden Stork

Bob Hite

Carl and Hilda Wildner

B-25B
Plane #11 (*Hari Carrier*)

U.S.S. Hornet (CV-8)

Runway of the training field (Auxiliary Field 1) used by the Raiders of the Eglin Field, Fla.

Raiders Annual Party in March 1991 in Carmel, Calif. Front row, left to right: Maj. Howard Sessler, Brig. Gen. Everett Holstrom, Brig. Gen. Richard Knobloch, Gen. Jimmy Doolittle, Maj. Gen. David Jones, Col. Henry Potter, Col. Robert Emmens. Back row, left to right: Col. William Bower, Maj. Thomas Griffin, Maj. Griff Williams, Capt. Royden Stork, Col. Travis Hoover, Staff Sgt. Jacob DeShazer, Tung-Sheng Liu, John Doolittle.

JOE RYCHETNIK, PACIFIC GROVE, CALIF.

ARMY, NAVY ISSUE STATEMENT, SCORING FALSE U.S. REPORTS

Planes Which Escaped to China Were All Seized by Japanese

'A PROPAGANDA ATTACK'

Futile Attempt to Disturb Morale Of People Called Amusing

The Army and Navy authorities on Thursday night made public a statement with regard to the air raids of American planes on the Japanese mainland on April 18 and their subsequent investigation. The statement follows:

"Judging from various information, enemy planes which attacked the Japanese mainland on April 18 were of the North American B-25 type and they numbered 10 and odds. They are supposed to have flown from an eastern ocean evidently for purposes of raiding the Keihin District, Nagoya, Kobe and Niigata, flying in formations of twos and threes or singly, and evidently with the intent of producing effects on nerve warfare.

"The United States, it is imagined, has attempted to circulate especially exaggerated news regarding the air raids, thereby trying to pacify the ever mounting outcries in that country against its successively adverse military operations and in an attempt to regain prestige in the eyes of its allies and third countries; particular with the intention of gaining popularity with Chungking, Australia and India. However, it can be well imagined to what extent the United States is worried over its predicament.

"Furthermore, simultaneously with scrutinizing the possibility of raiding the Japanese mainland, the enemy seemed to have attempted to supply airplanes to the Chungking regime, but the miserable failure of this scheme is amply testified by the following facts.

"At least two planes were almost definitely shot down in the vicinity of the Japanese mainland while several others were heavily damaged. Three additional craft were captured in Japanese occupied territories on the Chinese continent and moreover, those which escaped to unoccupied territories and barely managed to land, were immediately destroyed by the Japanese Air Units which lost no time in chasing the fleeing enemy craft.

"One American pilot succeeded in flying one plane into Soviet territory, but this can be looked upon only as a despicable act of attempting to stir up trouble in Japan-Soviet relation, and requires caution.

"If the American authorities hoped to disturb the Japanese people or to forestall the operations of the Imperial Forces on various southern fronts by an air raid on the Japanese mainland, then it is indeed amusing."

SEARCH FOR THE DOOLITTLE BOMBERS

by Bryan Moon

*In September 1990, an expedition, led by artist Bryan Moon of Frontenac, Minn.,
traveled to China to search for remains of aircraft Nos. 1, 3, 5, 10 and 11,
which crashed in the mountains of Zhejiang Province.*

FOR THE FOURTH CONSECUTIVE year, a hurricane had struck the coast of Zhejiang Province, 200 miles south of Shanghai. Flooding the fields and towns, 10,000 people took to the nearby mountains where the unrelenting rain washed out roads and bridges.

We arrived in Hangzhou, capital of the Province, in the wake of the storm. It was raining hard, much as it was 48 years earlier when 15 B-25 American bombers crashed into the mountains of Zhejiang Province.

Nothing had been seen of the bombers since that night of April 18, 1942.

Twelve months of research and work had preceded the 1990 Doolittle Raiders China Expedition's arrival in Hangzhou. It had come as a surprise to me that no one in the past 48 years had looked for the lost bombers. The surviving pilots and navigators of the Doolittle Raiders, to whom I wrote, were not optimistic that any parts of the aircraft could be found given the Chinese aptitude for making use of any available materials. But the crews willingly gave me coordinates of their bail-out locations from 1942, the direction their aircraft was flying at the time, altitude and other useful data. Gradually a plan developed around the approximate locations of five B-25 crash sites. Despite the pessimistic forecast, I became resolved to locate as many of the crash sites as possible and to retrieve any remnants of the aircraft that could be found.

The mountains of Zhejiang Province are not on the normal tourist routes of China. Indeed, I was later to learn that no foreigner had been in the area since 1942. The major obstacle was therefore to generate official approval from the Provincial Government for my Expedition to visit some of the more remote areas of the Province. Approval finally came one Friday evening in a telephone call from the People's Association for Friendship with Foreign Countries. It was followed by an official invitation in writing. The Expedition was on.

My Expedition colleagues shared a common interest in aviation, art and the outdoors. Joyce Olson was a vice president of a Publishing Company with expedition experience of primate research in Africa. Her daughter Heidi, the youngest member of the group, operated a health and fitness service. Doctor Tom Wier, a retired brigadier general from the U.S. Air Force Reserve was also an amateur aviation artist. From Britain, my close friend of many years, Arthur Gibson, was Europe's foremost aviation photographer. Representing the Doolittle Raiders was 72-year-old retired Colonel "Hank" Potter, the navigator on Doolittle's lead bomber in 1942. Better still, we had the blessings of the Doolittle Raiders who had graciously given the Expedition their name.

It became clear to me that approval once given, the Chinese felt committed to ensuring success of our mission. They dispatched ten field workers to various parts of the Province to plan our visit, accommodations, local transport and to check the villages nearest to the crash sites identified by surviving Raiders.

Despite the rain in Hangzou, we were anxious to get going. Our permanent escorts for the next 16 days were three representatives of the Association for Friendship with Foreign Countries. Our first search area was directly east of Hangzou in the Tianmu mountains. Jimmy Doolittle's aircraft had crashed on a mountain top in this region.

Hank Potter was remembering the night he had parachuted into space, injuring his ankle as he landed. His life had been saved by a young Chinese school teacher who spoke some English and who persuaded other villagers that the tall stranger was a friendly American flyer.

Our coach stopped at the town hall of Linan. As we stepped down, a not-so-young retired Chinese school teacher was reunited with Hank Potter, the American airman he had saved 48 years earlier. Zhu Xue-San was to stay with us for the next three days as we retraced his experiences of those war years so long past.

In 1942, the Chinese school teacher was 19 years old. He had graduated from secondary school and was teaching in primary school. The Japanese, who controlled most of the coast, had not come inland to his home near Linan. It was drizzling on the morning of April 19 when his breakfast was interrupted by the visit of two villagers who reported they had found two foreigners. The identity of the foreigners was a mystery to the villagers and only Mr. Zhu was likely to understand them.

Hank listened to the interpreter who was translating Mr. Zhu's memories. He too recalled being captured by villagers. With him at the time was Fred Braemer the bombardier. The villagers took their guns, wallets, watches and personal belongings. At knife and gun point, they were walked out into the rain. In the belief they were to be killed, the airmen tried to close the gap with the villagers, to recover their weapons and to fight their captors but without success. The young man of 19 came walking toward them.

When asked by the villagers to make contact with the foreigners, Mr. Zhu reacted, "I had a lot of worries. On one hand, my English was very poor. On the other hand, if I did not do that a misunderstanding was caused, there would be much worse big trouble. But when I saw them I said, 'Hello, how to do you do?' and the two foreigners were very happy. Before that they were frightened but once they knew someone was speaking English they were a little bit at ease." Mr. Zhu turned to the villagers and persuaded them to release the two fliers and to return to them their belongings. The two airmen then followed Mr. Zhu to his house where they enjoyed their first meal in China, hot tea and boiled eggs.

There is nothing on the mountain, we were told. The rain had made many of the roads impassable and our guides recommended against the climb. But of all the aircraft, Doolittle's was our first target and we had to see for ourselves. Three four-wheel-drive vehicles were hired to get us as close as possible to the crash site. As the clouds lifted a little, we finally came to a halt at the base of a very steep corn-covered mountainside.

A narrow path zig-zagged to the top and a group of fir trees amid thick bush. We reached the summit in a rain storm but there was nothing left of the bomber which had triggered the turning point of the Pacific war with Japan. We sheltered in the trees as the rain and high winds beat the hillside. It later eased long enough for our descent and we stood by the vehicles drinking Sprite and eating lunch. Our first search was a failure except for the fact that we were the only westerners to reach Doolittle's crash site since 1942.

The next morning, at the government office in the village of Qian Hong, we were met by local officials who steered us to a conference room. On the table lay a steel plate, clearly not from a propeller. Upon inspection it was identified as the armor plate from behind one of the pilot's seats. And since none of the other B-25's had crashed in this region, it had to come from Doolittle's aircraft. I negotiated a purchase and the last remnant of this historic aircraft was loaded onto the coach, the first prize of the Expedition. We were not far from the village of Baihe.

It was raining hard the night of April 18 when their first American visitor dropped from the skies at the edge of the village. Col. Jimmy Doolittle was the last to leave his aircraft. He described his experience.

"I was thinking about how I was going to land . . . in 1926 I had both legs broken in South America. The thing that disturbed me the most was whether my weak ankles would take a parachute drop. I decided that as soon as I landed I would sit down and in so doing minimize the load on my ankles and take some of it on my stern. I landed right in the middle of a rice paddy. I don't know whether you realize the time it takes a certain finite length of time to change your mind. I had made up my mind I was going to sit down and while I was in this rice paddy up to here, I sat down so that the water, a fertilizer, which is human excrement, came almost up to my neck. And while I was sitting down, the thought went through my mind, "Listen, stupid, you're all right, you don't have to sit down . . ." But I had already programmed the sit down and you can't change your mind instantaneously.

I got out of this as quick as I could and there was a house with a little light in the window. So I went over to the house and knocked on the door and said, "Lucia . . . something" which we had been assured was "I am an American." They promptly bolted the door and turned out the light.

Then I decided to try to find someplace to stay. It was raining very hard and the first place I found was a pair of sawhorses with a box about 8 ft. long, 3 ft. wide and about 2 ft. deep. And I thought well this is where I can get out of this rain. So I removed the lid, looked in, and there was a dead Chinaman in there. I abandoned that project and then found a little mill. This area was so primitive that they still had a paddlewheel and a creek to grind the rice, etc. That's where they put the stuff to be ground.

It was still raining like everything and there was water on the ground. I climbed into this thing to stay as dry as I could. I spent the night in and out of that thing because pretty soon I would get so cold being

Bryan Moon displays the armor plate panel from behind the pilot's seat of Doolittle's aircraft. The panel was originally found by a Chinese farmer living adjacent to the crash site in the West Tianmu Mountains, Zhejiang province. BRYAN MOON

wet completely through that I had to get up, jumping up and down and beat my arms. The next morning as soon as daylight came, I went looking for some help.

I found a chap carrying a yoke and two honey buckets. He didn't speak any English and I didn't speak any Chinese . . . so I tried to ask him where the railroad station was. He couldn't understand, so I got a little notebook out, drew him a picture of a railroad track and he indicated he understood what I wanted and he took me to the nearest military barracks and he turned me in. There was a young major there who spoke a little English. I immediately identified myself and he said "All right, if your story is true, could you go back to where you left your parachute." I said I could and we walked back to where I had left the parachute and it wasn't there.

We had already had a hell of an argument because I had maintained my .45. He wanted it immediately. I said, "No, one ally doesn't take another ally's sidearm." We'd had quite an argument about it and I wouldn't give it to him and he didn't want to take it by force. So we went back to look for this parachute. We couldn't find the parachute and things looked very bad for me. But one of the little Chinese soldiers went into the house and up on the back was a little elevated place where they kept stuff. He climbed up and looked back there and way in the corner was the parachute. Well, the minute the parachute was found, my story stood up and I was then taken to the governor of the province which was about half a day's walk."

We retraced Doolittle's steps. The village had grown since the war but the 18-year-old young man who first saw the man from the skies well remembered his meeting. Ji Zheng-fu also showed us the house at which Doolittle first sought shelter adding, "He knocked on this door but the farmers were frightened and would not come ot the door."

The time had come for us to move on. It's a four-hour drive to Shexian County in Anhui Province. At the border which separates Zhejiang and Anhui, Zhu Xue-san and Hank Potter embraced in a final farewell. We had entered a mountain range topping 5,000 feet. Somewhere up there in the trees were the remains of aircraft No. 11, but we had to be satisfied with locating the escape routes of the crew. A valley down which two crew members descended led to Xiad Zhou village where they were seen to read a map. A farmer approached them, took them first to the village school then to his house for a meal. We crossed the

A cap badge and razor belonging to a crew member of aircraft No. 3 found near the village of Beiyang. BRYAN MOON

same stone bridge to the farmer's house where his son Zhang Gen shan entertained us to tea. The son was 18 years old when he and his father fed the two American airmen and then guided them to Shexian. Time had not changed these kind, humble, gentle people. Yet they expressed such pride of our coming all the way from America to visit them.

The bus had been laboring up hill for nearly two hours. Since we left Suichang in the valley, a police car 50 yards ahead, forced oncoming traffic to a standstill as we crept past them on the narrow dirt road, whose crumbling edge spilled into the valley 1,000 feet below. The view was spectacular but unnerving for those on the outer seats of the bus. Our base for the next three days was a government hotel in the Jiou-long-san Nature Reserve, a three-story imposing stone building surrounded by mountains shrouded in mist.

The only surviving crew member of aircraft No. 3 was Charles Ozuk, the navigator. He had given me the coordinates of his parachute drop and the direction his aircraft had been flying. His briefing had been perfect and the aircraft had come to rest along the course he had plotted at an altitude of 5,500 feet near the village of Beiyang.

It was to take all day to reach the village, the hardest trek of our 16-day marathon. As we prepared for the day's climb, we must have shown some signs of fatigue to our escorts. With the exception of Heidi, the youngest member of our group, our average age was 62. Perhaps because of this, and knowing the difficulties of the climb ahead, our host suggested that some of us may prefer to be carried up the mountain in divan chairs adding, "the farmers are very strong." The offer was tempting but we were committed to making it under our own steam or not at all. Had we seen the mountain in advance, we may well have exhibited less bravado.

Beiyang was one of several small villages overlooking a sprawling valley itself more than 4,000 feet high. The terraced rice paddies and tea plantations spread across and along the lower slopes. It was a spectacular 360-degree panorama of great beauty. There was something very special about Beiyang.

The crew of Doolittle bomber No. 3 had other concerns on their mind when they parachuted over this same mountain valley nearly 50 years earlier. As the aircraft struck a peak two miles beyond the village, one member of the crew, Cpl. Leland Faktor, the engineer/gunner died in the crash.

The events of that fateful day were well known to two of the villagers, Huang fu gen and Huang fu hai. The interpreter translated for them, "And the next morning these two villagers found the crash site and laid the U.S. airman in the camp. They guarded the camp for two days and two nights. Then they carried the body to the village and later it was taken to Quzhou. For the remains of the aircraft, they asked seven or eight villagers to watch, to guard the remains. Then about seven days later, some officials from the government took the main part of the plane away."

It was a moving experience to retrace the events of 1942 in the simple translation of these gentle farmers. The story continued, "One villager was cutting grass. He found a big footprint and he traced the footprint and found another U.S. airman. He asked the airman to come with him to the village. At first, the airman was not so willing to come.

Two other villagers were also cutting grass in the mountain. They smelt the smoke of cigarettes and found the U.S. airmen. They came down the mountain to a river. They saw a raft near the river but there was not so much water so they could not do with the raft. They went down the mountain to a temple where they saw the portrait of the chairman of the government ruling China at that time. The airmen could recognize the portrait and saw that we were friends."

The head of the village invited us to follow him into another room. There, laid out on a table was an assortment of parts salvaged by the villagers from aircraft No. 3. Among them were the most personal prizes of the Expedition, an officer's cap badge and a razor, both in remarkable condition. Among the mementos was a large round bowl and a scoop with a hole in it. Puzzled by these exhibits which were clearly not aircraft parts, the interpreter explained that villagers had fashioned these items from sections of aircraft aluminum. The purchase negotiations were short and I readily agreed to the price they asked for all the items of the table. All but one.

The section of armor plate measured nearly 53″ by 20″ and must have weighed over 300 pounds. It was much larger than the section of steel we had retrieved from Doolittle's aircraft but identical in all other respects. But from which part of the aircraft had it come? And how would we manhandle such a heavy and unyielding item? "The farmers will carry it down the mountain if you want it," said the interpreter. We had nearly half the search program ahead of us and the steel plate in our crowded bus could be more of a hazard than a prize. Reluctantly, it was left behind, perhaps for some future expedition to rescue.

The crash site of No. 3 was another two miles up yet another mountainside. Four of us were given village-made walking sticks and we set out for the summit. We were told the farmers had placed seats on the mountain top for us to rest, yet another example of the consideration and kindness extended to us by all the Chinese people. It was hotter now and I was beginning to feel the effects of not eating for two days plus the long hard climb to Beiyang. We were ten minutes from the top and within sight of the trees that had sheltered Corporal Faktor's body after the crash. One of the guides picked up a piece of aluminum, which must have come from No. 3 aircraft. Later, I mounted this section onto a plaque and presented it to Corporal Faktor's brother, a promise I had made if any part of No. 3 aircraft was found.

Two of the airmen from No. 3 aircraft had parachuted into the slopes near Xiban and had found shelter in the village. These same airmen then walked down the valley to Liu-jia village where they hid under a bridge.

In the town hall we met the two men who first found the airmen under the bridge, Liou Fanqiao and Liou Guan-xiong. Liou Fanqiao had taken the airmen to the town hall where they had rested for three days and three nights. The interpreters continued, "Well, the story goes like this. At first the father of Liou Fanqiao prepares some rice for the U.S. airmen, but the U.S. airmen do not like to eat rice. His father took out a pen and a piece of paper and drew a chicken. The U.S. airmen nodded their heads. And then they prepared some chicken and some eggs to eat. Also the airman's coat was very ditry and there was blood was on it, so his father asked the airman to take off his clothes so they could be washed. Mr. Liou Fanqiao's father lent his own clothes for the U.S. airman to wear but the airman was very tall. His father's clothes were too short for him. Three days later, his father asked Mr. Liou Fanqiao to escort the airmen to Shanting, the headquarters of the district.

"At that time, they had to walk through the mountains in order to reach Shanting. The U.S. airman was badly wounded on the back, so he stopped several times on the way. And Mr. Liou Fanqiao helped him a lot on the way to Shanting. The airman carried with him a gun and he asked Mr. Liou Fanqiao if he would carry it for him as he was wounded at that time. Mr. Liou Fanqiao carried it for him. When they reached Shanting, they over-nighted and the next morning they had to say good-bye to each other. And the U.S. airmen brought out two U.S. coins with Washington's portrait on them and gave them to Mr. Liou Fanqiao as a souvenir."

Lt. Ted Lawson, captain of the RUPTURED DUCK, number seven off the Hornet's carrier deck, was low on fuel as his B-25 bomber approached the coast of China. He chose to ditch the aircraft in the shallow water bay of an offshore island. The aircraft hit the water hard causing four of the five-man crew to be badly injured. In the dark, they struggled to reach shore. The island was Nantien. It was in a Japanese-controlled area. Not far way, a second B-25 was ditching close to the neighboring island of Tan Tou Shan. Number 15 aircraft made a smooth landing, remaining afloat for several minutes while the crew, unhurt, inflated a life raft and headed for shore. The gunner Lt. Thomas R. White, was also a physician. Dr. White was to later play a major role in treating the injured crew of aircraft number seven. Unknown to the crew of number 15 aircraft, they had also landed in Japanese occupied territory.

We were not permitted to visit Nantien Island, it being a military-controlled zone. But we were anxious to learn more of the circumstances surrounding the escape of crew No. 7, and also of crew No. 15, whose aircraft was ditched near Tan Tou Shan Island next to Nantien. Our Chinese hosts had therefore brought from the islands, four representatives of the fishing villages, three men and a lady.

Wang Xiao-fu, age 75 and Xu Shang-brao, age 78, both had lived in Dasha village on Nantien Islannd all their lives. As they spoke of April 18, the interpreter translated for us.

"The weather was terrible because the storm was just over. At that time there was an aircraft coming over the village and circled around for a time and going back over the ocean. Then it splashed into the water about 1,000 meters from the shore. When the aircraft crashed, they wanted to help and one of the villagers was Mr. Xu Shang-brao. He helped one of the U.S. airmen from the water to the shore. Among the five crew members, four were badly injured. One was just okay. They couldn't walk themselves so the villagers carried them and supported them to walk. They took the airmen to the primary school and there they cooked meals for them. But some were not used to Chinese dish, so instead of rice they cooked eggs. And early next morning, the villagers used a door and blanket to make a stretcher and carried the U.S. airmen to the top of the mountain. Mr. Wang Xiao fu is one of the people who helped carry them to the top of the mountain.

"The situation was very complicated. Nantien was occupied by the Japanese so the local villagers just risked their lives rescuing the U.S. airmen. At the top of the mountain, the U.S. airmen were handed over to the 1st Division (of the Chinese army). During the sending of the airmen to the local headquarters, the 1st Division and villagers fought back. Mr. Thatcher the Engineer-Gunner was not too badly wounded and joined in the fighting. The U.S. airmen got to headquarters at 12 o'clock on the 20th and they were treated and given a warm welcome.

"On the morning of the 21st, all the airmen were escorted to Linhai for further treatment. There were two reasons for that. On the one hand, this place bordered on the area occupied by the Japanese. It is not good policy to let the U.S. airmen stay here for a long time. On the other hand, the conditions in the local clinic was very poor."

The conversation returned to the scene of the crash. "The aircraft crashed into Nantien Island and exploded in two parts. The Japanese sent a ship to take it away. The local villagers were afraid of the Japanese very much. They would beat you. They killed all their chickens . . . for their meals. The Japanese soldiers did not disassemble the aircraft themselves, the local villagers were made to do that. They were hit on the back of the head very hard. Fortunately, the U.S. airmen were sent to Sanmen at an early date. Otherwise, if the Japanese found them, all the families of the fishermen would be killed."

Our disappointment at not being permitted to visit Nantien was tempered by the accounts of the two fishermen. As their story ended and without ceremony, they passed two objects across the table. One was a small circular metal bowl with two threaded apertures at its base. The other was a scoop made by the aircraft aluminum. We had been given the last remaining artifacts of a bomber which was to be further immortalized in the book and later the movie *30 Seconds Over Tokyo* written by Lt. Ted Lawson.

We turned to the lady and the fourth fisherman who had come from Tai Tou Shan Island, anxious to hear of their experiences of a time long since past. The handsome Chinese lady Zhao Xiao-bao looked far younger than her 67 years. When the olive green bomber ditched near her island, she was 19 years old. She and her husband, like 65-year-old Lin Fu-sou who sat next to her across the table, had lived quietly in Da Wang-gong village on the shore of Tai Tou Shan Island. The

Japanese occupation of their island had changed their peaceful lives and the night of April 18 had unexpectedly introduced yet another greater element of danger.

The interpreters were doing a good job and while their English was not perfect, their impromptu translations made the stories more spontaneous and natural.

"And now we go to the story of the other aircraft. The other aircraft splashed into the ocean which is 500 meters to the village of Da Wang-gong. The ocean which the aircraft splashed into was very deep so the aircraft sank to the bottom, but the airmen bailed out. Thanks to the early bailing out, all of them were safe. No problem. One of them got slightly wounded. At that stage, four of the airmen got to the seashore and one of them was missing. These four people walked in the direction of the village with the help of flashlights. Seeing the flashlights, the local villagers took it for granted that they were, sort of bandits or the Japanese invaders.

"So the villagers were worried too much and they moved to the mountain to get into hiding. And staying in the mountains for several days, the villagers found nothing happened and gradually they came down the mountains and they found the four U.S. airmen hiding in, sort of a pig pen, in front of this lady's home. When her husband got home, he saw a shadow near the pig pen and he used a flashlight and found the U.S. airmen in there. The reason why the U.S. airmen were hiding was because, during their hurry–escape to the mountains–Mr. Zhao forgot to extinguish the light and so the U.S. airmen thought there must be someone at home.

"After seeing the foreigners, they knew they were not the Japanese because these people were very tall and high nose. But they couldn't tell which country they came from and Mr. Zhao (the lady's husband) took them to his home. She also was at home. Mr. Zhao couldn't speak any English so he could not make himself understood by the airmen and so in order to get understanding he asked for help from the primary school teacher but unfortunately the primary school teacher did not speak English either, so they figured out a way by drawing pictures.

"At first, they drew a Japanese flag and all four foreigners were very angry. And after that the Chinese flag, and the four foreigners were smiling and shake hands with the teacher. Mr. Lin Fu-sou was also present at that time. And following that, the foreigners took out a map and laid out the map on a table and pointed in the direction of the United States so that the local villagers knew that they were from America. After knowing the foreigners were American they just gave as much help as possible. They fire the wood to dry their clothes. They cook the meals for them to eat. On that evening all the four U.S. airmen were accommodated at the lady's home.

"The next morning on the 19th, the four U.S. airmen went out in search for their colleague for he was missing. They found him in the mountains at last. There was an emotional moment when they found their missing colleague. They embraced each other, just chatting with each other, just emotional. And returning to Mr. Zhao's home all the five U.S. airmen asked the villagers either to send them to Chungking, the headquarters of the commandant, or to the local headquarters at Sanmen, which was an island next to where they were. They had a discussion and decided to send the U.S. airmen to Sanmen. After lunch, they got a small boat and transpoted the U.S. airmen to a beach which was just near, past our village. When they sent the U.S. airmen out they made up disguise for the sake of safety. When they got to the

shore, they were taken away by guerrillas. The U.S. airmen were sheltered in a secret place called Wang Li Dong cave.

"The U.S. airmen hid in the Wang Li Dong cave in the daytime, and in the evening the guerrillas wanted to transport them. They got a boat. The guerrillas wanted to transport them to Sanmen. On the way they were attacked by the Japanese soldiers and they had no way but to retreat to Baihe San cave. At that stage, a Japanese warship came to the foot of the mountain for the U.S. airmen. Fortunately, the U.S. airmen hid at the top of the mountain and escaped from the Japanese. Through hardship on the 21st, they were moved and at four p.m. that day they finally got to Sanmen county. When the U.S. airmen reached the local headquarters of Sanmen county they were treated very well and the local villagers had made coats for them.

"On the morning of the 23rd a grand farewell was held. On the streets, all the kids were lined up with flowers and they felt sorry for the departing of the U.S. airmen. The U.S. airmen felt moved by this conduct on this occasion and they made a speech. And they asked the local government to send them to Linhai. They, the airmen on the first aircraft we talked about (No. 7), were also carried to Linhai by sedan chair. The situation in 1942 was very complicated. It was a time we were struggling very hard against the Japanese aggression."

The crews of both ditched aircraft, she¬hered through Japanese lines by Chinese guerrillas finally came together at Linhai, a town 20 miles inland from the coast and bordering on the Japanese-controlled territories. Linhai provided a facility especially needed by the crew of number seven aircraft–a hospital.

We were nearing the end of our search and a visit to Taizhou hospital in Linhai was to be an all-day affair. The modest facility in which Doctor Cheng Sheng-yan had amputated Lt. Lawson's battered leg and attended to his crew, had grown into the Province's largest hospital. The 700 staff members included 50 surgeons. With 520 beds, the hospital provided medical care for more outpatients and we were appalled to learn that the daily patient count average 2,000.

It was Dr. Cheng's father who, in 1932, had purchased a dispensary run by a Christian church and turned it into Taizhou Hospital. Ten years later an American bomber crew was to find sanctuary and the life-saving skills of the founder's son. The small size and quiet demeanor of the doctor was disarming, but this was the same man who had risked his life to save the American airmen. He read to us in broken English a prepared statement and generously posed for video and still pictures. Hank presented a plaque signed by all 44 surviving Raiders in recognition and appreciation of the doctor's contribution in the events following the assault on Japan.

Our circuitous search pattern finally ended where it had begun in Hangzhou. The evening meal was to be a formal farewell dinner hosted by senior Chinese officials of the Province. For the first time, we dressed formally, the men with ties and suits or sports coats, the ladies in dresses.

We were greeted by Mr. Zhao Jia-fu, director of the Provincial Foreign Affairs Department, to whom Hank presented the plaque. After the speches, we talked with two elderly Chinese gentlemen who had come to Hangzhou to meet with us. Before the evening was over, we were to hear of their role in rescuing members of aircraft No. 11.

Lt. Kenneth E. Reddy was co-pilot of the Hari-Kari-er, the 11th air craft to take off from the Hornet. *After fourteen and a half hours, at*

Plaque presented to officials of Zhejiang Province signed by the 44 surviving Raiders. The plaque bears an inscription that reads, in part: "Most of the airmen who took part in the raid survived, thanks to the courage and self-sacrifice of the Chinese people who sheltered them from the Japanese. On behalf of all of the American airmen of the Doolittle Tokyo Raiders, the survivors who have signed this remembrance express their gratitude to the people of China for their courage and for the personal sacrifices of so many in 1942."

10,000 feet over China, the Hari-Kari-er had five to fifteen minutes of fuel remaining. The automatic pilot was engaged and the crew assembled in the area immediately behind the pilots' seats. The door to navigator's compartment was dropped off. It was 10:30 p.m. Lt. Reddy's diary reads, "Lt. Frank Kappeler the navigator, S.Sgt. William Birch the bombardier and S.Sgt. Melvin J. Gardner the engineer/gunner stood around the open door waiting for the word to jump from Captain C. Ross Greening.

It was to be nearly 36 hours before they were to meet again. Separated in the parachute drop, Reddy's head was bleeding. He spent a wet and sleepless night on the mountain before walking the next day down a stream to a village where he met Captain Greening. An interpreter in the village assured their acceptance and they were fed and housed. The next day, Lt. Kappeler was brought in then Birch and Gardner. They were all led across a 300-year-old bridge where they posed for pictures, then loaded onto a truck for the drive to Chusien and safety.

Mr. Zeng Jian-pei was a distinguished looking gentleman. He and Mr. Wei Han-min had come from Shanghai to meet with us. Mr. Zeng was the young interpreter who had met Greening and Reddy. He pointed to Mr. Wei as he said, "It was he who fetched Captain Greening, Lt. Reddy and Lt. Kappeler on a postal truck all the way to Chusien." Mr. Wei was now a retired former Inspector of Field Post Offices. Greening's diary had referred to him as the rather intelligent young man."

Mr. Zeng was clear in his memories of 1942. "In three or four days, I met Lt. Joyce (Captain of aircraft No. 10). Joyce had intercepted the picture taken on the bridge of Greening's crew, one of the few historic photographs of the Doolittle Raiders in China.

Mr. Zeng had accompanied Mr. Wei, Greening, Reddy and Kappeler to Chusien. While the airmen were being treated in the hospital, Mr. Zeng elicited that two of the crew members, Birch and Gardner were missing. Mr. Zeng and Mr. Wei then returned in the postal vehicle to look for the other airmen. They found Bush and Gardner in the village.

Birch was washing his feet when Mr. Zeng asked him what else he could do. Birch asked for a bottle of Shanghai beer. Mr. Zeng recalled his reaction, "I thought it was really . . . to get a bottle of beer in time of war!" Nearly 48 years passed in which time no one could recall whether the beer was forthcoming. Finally Mr. Zeng received a letter from Lt. Kappeler saying that a bottle of beer was found for Sgt. Birch.

The two airmen were driven in the postal vehicle and reunited with their colleagues in Chusien. Another of the Doolittle crews had been saved.

In a final ceremony, Hank Potter presented plaques and American flag pins to Mr. Wei and Mr. Zeng. The expedition was over. We had met and honored the Chinese people to whose courage 44 American owed their lives. We had sought the remains of five of the Doolittle bombers and found three. It was time to go home. The day we left China, Hank celebrated his seventy-third birthday.

Moon's China Expedition Makes Unexpected Discoveries

A 19-man expedition returned from its expedition to China in April 1994 with artifacts they had not originally planned to find. Led by Minnesota artist Bryan Moon, their first week was spent on a 180-ton steel launch trailing sonar gear in search of a sunken B-25 bomber from the famous 1942 raid on Japan. One aircraft, the 15th to take off from the carrier *Hornet*, was the only bomber to land intact, coming down on the coastal waters near Tan Toushan Island, about 150 miles south of Shanghai.

The search covered an area of water one and one-third miles long by three-quarters of a mile wide. Forty-eight passes, each one and one-third miles long concentrated on the area of the bomber's landing. The location was determined in part from a map provided by the surviving copilot of No. 15 bomber and confirmed by an elderly fisherman from the island. The expedition members were the first Americans to land on Tan Toushan since Doolittle bomber No. 15's crew paddled ashore on April 18th, from their sinking aircraft. They hid in the pig pen of the Zhao Xiaobao's family house where they were fed, sheltered and hidden from the searching Japanese. Expedition members retraced the airmen's path to the point they had landed on the island.

Despite an exhaustive search and diving by Gerry Provost of Plymouth, MN, and Rick Wadle of San Antonio, TX, no trace of Doolittle bomber No. 15 was found. The divers reported a deep mud floor. Islanders said that six typhoons had hit their coast in the past 18 months. The expedition concluded that the famous warbird was battered to pieces by 52 years of high winds and strong currents and has since sunk into the mud.

The search program was not without its tense moments. With the mother ship unable to get close into the rocky shore, a small fishing boat took six expedition members close into the coastline. In turbulent weather conditions and strong winds, the engine cut. Without an anchor on board, the small boat quickly drifted toward the rocks as expedition members fastened life jackets. Fifty feet from the rocks, the Chinese boatman persuaded the engine into life but it died again shortly after. The crew was rescued by a passing Chinse fishing boat that towed them back to the mother ship.

Expedition director Bryan Moon decided to abandon the search after the first week, confident that the sonar and divers would have found the aircraft had it still rested above the muddy floor of the China Sea. Their first unexpected discovery, however, was made the following day.

The expedition's Chinese hosts had gathered eleven elderly veterans who had rescued Doolittle airmen from three B-25s. A public ceremony to honor these veterans was conducted with Col. "Hank" Potter, Doolittle's navigator, officiating for the expedition. One of the honorees was an elderly lady who had been involved in the recovery of two airmen from Doolittle bomber No. 6, killed in the crash landing of their aircraft. She unexpectedly produced a parachute harness release that had come from one of the two dead airmen. Col. Potter examined the artifact and confirmed its 1942 authenticity. Moon then negotiated its purchase from the elderly lady.

The expedition took an unscheduled course that was to lead to another discovery. Expedition member George Eisele, a marketing executive from New Jersey, tabled a magazine article entitled *The shooting down of Admiral Yamagata*, the 1945 air battle that ended the life of one of Japan's most important military officers. The story focused on a Japanese Emily Flying Boat that was carrying the admiral back to Japan when it was intercepted by a B-24 U.S. patrol bomber and forced to land in a river near the town of Linhai. Coincidentally the expedition was en route to Linhai where Dr. Chen Shenyan had administered medical attention to the crew of No. 15 and No. 7 bombers. The latter was captained by Ted Lawson, who later wrote *30 Seconds Over Tokyo*. Lawson's leg was critically injured in his aircraft's crash landing and was amputated at Linhai hospital, an action that saved his life.

With the crash site of the Emily so near, but with a complicated series of reunion programs remaining, the Chinese agreed that two members of the expedition could be diverted to research the crashed Japanese Emily Flying Boat. The expedition director's son, Christopher Moon, a business owner from Bloomington, MN, and diver/underwater video director Rick Wadle of San Antonio, TX, left the group and headed for a fishing village at the river's mouth where the Emily had been forced down.

It was March 17, 1945, when the Kawanishi four-engined Emily transport was intercepted off the coast of China. Fifty-four-year-old Admiral Saigo Yamagata was returning to Japan from his command of the western Pacific war zone to become under-secretary of the Imperial Japanese Navy. Eleven crew members and 22 passengers were aboard the Emily converted Patrol Flying Boat. Plans for the secret flight had been intercepted and deciphered by U.S. Navy cryptologists. U.S. Naval Intelligence, therefore, knew the admiral's schedule and directed a series of armed reconnaissance missions to locate and shoot down the Emily. The B-24 captained by Lt. Paul Stevens first saw the Emily off the coast of China and promptly closed in to attack. The Emily was raked by machine gun fire and forced to land in the river near Linhai. All the crew were killed or captured by Chinese guerrillas and the admiral committed seppuku (suicide) after the Flying Boat was set afire and later sank.

At the fishing village near the Emily's last seen location, Chris Moon and Rick Wadle located elderly local citizens who had seen the Emily in 1945. In a loaned fisherman's boat with five Chinese volunteers armed with 10-foot bamboo poles, the search team was guided into position over the sunken aircraft by villagers from the shore waving directions. The poles were then driven down into the mud to feel out the submerged aircraft. But once positioned, suction from the mud made it impossible to raise the poles, much to the amusement of the Chinese onlookers.

Not to be outdone, the intrepid pair of expedition members turned their attention to seeking aircraft remains being held by fishermen. The village square offered a likely homemade billboard location. Equipped with a wood panel, paint and brushes, their interpreter painted a sign inviting villagers with remains of the Emily to call a hotel number. A crowd gathered to watch the painting and billboard positioning in the village square. It was learned that one villager had such an artifact and negotiations over two days with family members resulted in the sale of a 3½″ long metal pipe section later identified as a muffler exhaust manifold from one of the Flying Boat's four 1850 hp Mitsubishi engines. Engraved Japanese characters in the unit are probably part numbers. These will be photographically

enlarged for analysis via Mitsubishi. Expedition member Tom Crane's Plymouth company, T. Crane & Associates, will further analyze the metal.

Both the pilot of the B-24 that intercepted the admiral's Flying Boat and a Japanese crew member are alive. Expedition director and aviation artist, Bryan Moon, plans to reunite both airmen for the signing of a commemorative print of the 1945 action. A cutting from the only remaining artifact will be affixed to each print.

Moon summarized the expedition as a great experience for all the members, who worked harmoniously throughout the search programs. Determining the fate of the Doolittle bomber and making the two unexpected discoveries made the experience rewarding and, most importantly, all the members came back safely and in good health.

TOP: The nearly deserted town on Tan Toushan Island where the crew of No. 15 bomber were hidden from the Japanese.
BOTTOM: Nine Chinese veterans, all of whom helped to rescue the Raiders. Each is wearing a medallion of gratitude presented to them by Moon's expedition during a special ceremony. Madam Zhao, who rescued the crew, is fourth from the right.
STORY AND PHOTOS COURTESY BRYAN MOON, FRONTENAC, MINNESOTA

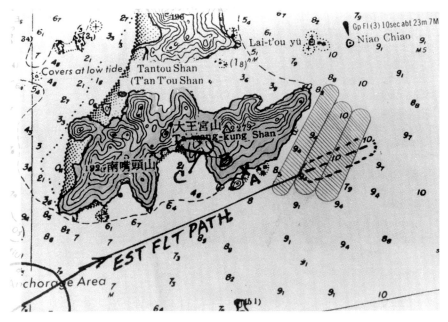

The original map of Tan Toushan Island on which No. 15 bomber's flight path was marked by co-pilot Major Griffith Williams. The cross-hatched portion is the search area covered by the expedition.

The original home of Madam Zhao on Tan Toushan Island in which the crew were sheltered, fed and hidden from the Japanese. Madam Zhao's son stands in front.

A parachute harness release worn by a crew member of No. 6 bomber anda held by the Chinese lady who re-moved it from the airman's body.

~~SECRET~~ Directive No. 3-31

WAR DEPARTMENT
HEADQUARTERS OF THE ARMY AIR FORCES
Washington

January 13, 1942

DIRECTIVE MEMO FOR: A-3

Subject: Carrier Type of B-25's.

1. Three B-25's with excellent crews will be sent to Norfolk to arrive January 20th for carrier tests. These tests will be to determine the take-off characteristics of the B-25. One of the carriers will be made available at that place and tests will be conducted as follows:

1st plane take-off lightly loaded
2nd plane take-off with a medium load, and
3rd plane with a full load.

Successive take-offs will, of course, be gauged by the preceding ones. A thoroughly capable Army Air Force officer of experience will supervise these tests.

2. Prepare a memo to Admiral King for General Arnold's signature outlining in brief this plan.

By direction of the Chief of the Air Staff.

[signature]

C. E. Duncan,
Lieut. Colonel, Air Corps,
Secretary of the Air Staff.

MEMORANDUM FOR RECORD:

Air Force Combat Command notified by telephone. Directive to Air Force Combat Command and Memorandum for Admiral King for General Arnold's signature forwarded from A-3 on Jan. 14, 1942.

DECLASSIFIED
DOD ltrs.
8 Jan & 20 June 1974
By: [signature] 12/30/75

for [signature: Vandenberg]
EARL L. NAIDEN
Colonel, Air Corps,
Chief A-3 Division.

CS/cmc

~~SECRET~~

These two rare photos show B-25 bombers at the Mid-Continent Airlines modification center at Wold-Chamberlin Field in Minneapolis, Minnesota. Extra fuel tanks were installed along with 24 high-pressure valves into the hydraulic line, pilot seat back armor and additional consumption, cruise control and range charts. Note the guard by the plane. COURTESY MARK COPELAND, BLOOMINGTON, MINNESOTA

Wade B. Campbell Remembers The Day

On April 8, 1941, I joined the U.S. Navy in Columbia, South Carolina, two days after my seventeenth birthday. After boot camp in Norfolk, Virginia, I attended Aviation Machinist Mate School at the Naval Air Station in Jacksonville, Florida. Upon graduation, I was assigned to Squadron Scouting 8, U.S. Navy Air Group 8, which was training to go aboard the newest U.S. Navy aircraft carrier USS Hornet (CV-8), which was to be commissioned on October 20, 1941. I was a plane-captain on Plane #S-8, although only 17 at the time.

While training, we participated in the Red and Blue War Games maneuvers in the Carolinas during the fall of 1941. After the commissioning of the ship, we were at sea most of the time on "shake down" cruises and training to land our aircraft on the ship's deck, etc.

On Sunday, December 7, 1941, we were in port for liberty at the Naval Base in Norfolk. An announcement was made on the local radio stations for all hands to return to ship immediately as soon as the Pearl Harbor attack was known. Back on board, we continued to train and within the first days of February 1942, two B-25s were on the dock at the Naval Air Station in Norfolk and they were loaded aboard. We went to sea and launched the first twin engine aircraft ever from a U.S. Naval aircraft carrier. The planes did not return to the ship, but went back to a land base. The launching of the aircraft had gone smoothly.

Our planes to this point were SBC-4s (Curtis bi-planes), which were already obsolete.

During March 1942, we passed through the Panama Canal and made port in San Diego, California. It was the first time the USS Hornet CV-8 had been out of the Atlantic. We had previously gotten a few SBD-4s (Douglas dive bombers) for our pilots to learn and practice dive bombing and landing on the carrier deck. We picked up more SBDs in San Diego, disassembled the wings and various parts so that everything could be hung in the overhead of the hangar deck. Our four squadrons—Fighting 8, Torpedo 8, Bombing 8, and Scouting 8—each had eighteen planes, which were now in the loft and on the floor of the hangar deck; our flight deck was cleared.

After pulling out of San Diego, we arrived at the Alameda Naval Air Station, San Francisco Bay, on April 1 and began loading 16 B-25s, with cranes, onto the flight deck. (This was shown in the movie "Thirty Seconds Over Tokyo.") On the night of April 1, some of us were granted liberty. A baker, Earl Whitt, and I hitchhiked to San Jose to see his sister and her family. Every car that picked us up asked the same question: "Do you think the Japanese are going to invade California?"

"There is nothing," these people kept saying, "to keep the Japanese from coming right on in and taking the coast, except the protection that some citizens have of privately owned guns."

The fear ws genuine because of the general knowledge that we were in no way prepared for a war and even less protected since the destruction at Pearl Harbor. In fact, some of the machine gun barrels on B-24s were broom handles—so desperate a hurry to make this raid on Japan had precluded waiting for weapons to be made. The fact, of course, was unknown to most.

After pulling out of San Francisco Bay the morning of April 2, 1942, and getting well out to sea, we began betting on where we were headed. Where would be our next liberty port? I thought, because of the short range of flight for the B-25, we were probably ferrying these planes down near Australia so they could fly to a base somewhere in the South Pacific. Then the announcement came over the loud speakers that our mission was to take these planes and crews as close as possible to Japan without being sighted and launch the first bombing raid on Japan. It was a jolting, overwhelming thought for so many of us "swabbies" who were still in our teens, but we were ready to help strike back for those who were lost at Pearl Harbor.

The Doolittle Raiders, we learned, would then fly to China to land. We also learned that Admiral "Bull" Halsey was in command of this mission and that he was aboard the USS Enterprise CV-7, and that ship's squadrons would be providing the task force with fighting and scouting air protection. Cruisers and destroyers were also in the group.

Everything was going smoothly until the morning of April 18. We had made every effort to teach the Army Air Force men aboard how to play poker—with a profit to the sailors during the cruise to launch. We were at general quarters that morning with all our hatches battened down and I was returning through the port holes from the bake shop. While eating a few doughnuts and climbing the ladder on the port side of the ship, between the hangar and flight decks, I heard the USS Nashville—a light cruiser—begin firing its 5-inch guns. At the rate of about ten steps each stride, I arrived on the flight deck and saw the water settle on the horizon and some Japanese fishing boats or trawlers sinking. At this point, an air of anxiety settled as the thought came to all of us that the Japanese mainland might now be aware of our location.

Plans were to launch the raiders late that afternoon, April 18, and have a night raid on Japan. The plans changed after Admiral Halsey and (then) Colonel Doolittle decided to proceed immediately with the launch.

The ocean was rough and winds were high. The bow of our ship was dipping into the sea. The flagmen, who had to signal the planes when to take off, had to start the planes rolling at precisely the right second so that the bow would be pointed up instead of into the water when they left the deck. Colonel Doolittle's plane was the first to go. The others took off without incident until the last plane—whose tail was now hanging over the fantail of the ship. A Petty Officer had been on the deck to remove the chock from the nose wheel when another plane at mid-ship was revving its engines at full throttle, preparing to be signaled for takeoff. The wind from the revving propellers, plus the strong wind blowing down the deck, pushed the sailor into one of the moving propellers of that last plane. I watched what looked to be an impossible situation as the sailor bravely ▶

stood and fought against all odds facing him, and lost his arm, although it could have been his life.

As Doolittle's Raiders flew into their destiny, we were getting our planes assembled, heading toward the Coral Sea, a return to Pearl Harbor, and Midway with action in between—six months of other events, but our final destiny was tied to Doolittle's Raiders.

On October 20th, about six months after we launched Doolittle's Raiders, we were eating our birthday dinner—the USS *Hornet* was one year old—when general quarters sounded: "MAN YOUR BATTLE STATIONS." A Japanese patrol plane had been sighted by our fighter planes and we saw the smoke as the plane came down. While finishing our dinner, we were told that the Japanese had learned that the Doolittle Raiders were launched from our deck and the command went out to sink the "Blue Base"—the *Hornet's* code name—at all cost.

Six days later, on October 26, 1942, Japanese planes began attacking the ship around eight o'clock in the morning. During the first twenty minutes of the attack, we received suicide planes, bombs, and torpedoes. Our main engine room was flooded and we were laid-to in the water fighting fires. The attacks lasted all day—and we were forced to abandon ship late that evening. The U.S. destroyers completed the job of sinking the ship that night because we were in Japanese territory.

The U.S. Navy announced the sinking of the *Hornet* in January 1943 and the report confirmed that we had shot down 156 planes the day the ship was sunk. There was no doubt, the USS *Hornet* CV-8 was the target that day.

When President Roosevelt had announced the successful raid on Japan, he was asked where the planes came from and had replied, "Shangri-la." When the USS *Hornet* CV-8 was sunk, the President ordered that a keel CV-12 already laid have the name changed to USS *Hornet* CV-12. He also ordered another aircraft carrier be named *Shangri-la.*

Although the penalty to the USS *Hornet* CV-8 was death-at-sea for its part in the Doolittle Raid, two ships carried on the name.

—WADE B. CAMPBELL, *Greenville, South Carolina*

WAR DEPARTMENT
HEADQUARTERS OF THE ARMY AIR FORCES
WASHINGTON

January 22, 1942

MEMORANDUM FOR THE CHIEF OF THE AIR STAFF.

Subject: B-25 Alterations.

1. In compliance with verbal instructions received from General Arnold, it is requested that one B-25B airplane be made available to the Mid-Continent Airlines at Minneapolis, Minnesota on January 23, 1942, or at the earliest possible moment thereafter. It is further requested that 17 more B-25B's be diverted to the Mid-Continent Airlines for alteration as required. The undersigned will advise A-3 when these airplanes are required.

J. H. Doolittle,
Lieut. Colonel, Air Corps.

Objective in Japan Most Desirable for Attack.

General   General   1942   **Attention A-2**
Arnold   Spaatz   1/22

It is desired that you select for me the objectives
in Japan you consider most desirable to be attacked in case
we find it possible to send bombardment airplanes over
Japan sometime in the near future. The bombing mission
should be able to cover any part of Japan from Tokyo south.

H. H. A.

The Doolittle Raiders monument was placed at the U.S. Air Force Museum in Dayton, Ohio, in 1988.

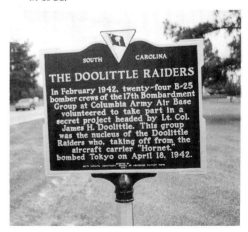

Sign at the Columbia, South Carolina, airport.

The following photos from Roy Stork's Collection are now deposited at the Travis AFB Museum Archives.

Training field scenes from Eglin Field, Florida.

Above: Some of the crew in their Eglin Field barracks.

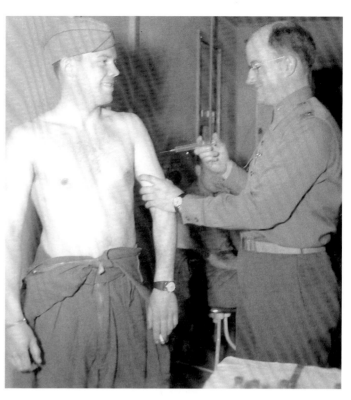

*Right: Dick Joyce getting his shots
from Dr. White at Eglin Field.*

*Short takeoff
training
within
650 feet.*

The crew of No. 7 in China. From left: a Chinese doctor, Robert Clever, Dean Davenport, Ted Lawson, Charles McClure and Dr. Thomas White (not on the crew but was the gunner on No. 15 and operated on Lawson's leg). Crewmember Dave Thatcher had already left China when photo was taken.

Crewmen loading on a boat on their way to a rendezvous point to fly out of China.

Hilger and crew.

Crew with Chinese soldiers.
From left: Jack Sims, Jimmy Doolittle, John Hilger.

Hilger and a Chinese general.

This photo was taken just before some of the raiders left for Chenschin, China. Front row from left: Horace Crouch, Thadd Blanton, Chinese magistrate, Ed Horton, Roy Stork. Back row from left: William Pound, Bill Bower, Waldo Bither, Omer Duquette.

Left: Roy Stork in front of magistrate's home. Above: Crew of No. 14 in China. From left: Ed Bain, Jacob Eierman, Jack Sims, John Hilger, James Macia.

First group to leave China.

The first group boarding a C-47.

Second group to leave China.

Wirephoto: Jimmy Doolittle Discloses "Shangri-La" Base to Gang of Bomber Builder

Wirephoto: Addressing the men and women who helped build the B-25 bombers which he led in the first bombing raid on Japan, Brigadier General Jimmie Doolittle (speaking) at Inglewood, Calif., yesterday located the mythical base Shangri-La as right in the North American Aviation pla Doolittle praised the planes and their builders' work. (AP

This photo was taken the day before the U.S.S. Hornet *left for the mission, April 1, 1942. From left: Horace Crouch, Roy Stork, Dick Joyce.*

Roy Stork, on leave in 1943 after 16 months in the C.B.I. Theater of Operations, visited the Hollywood set of the movie Goverment Girl, *starring Olivia de Havilland. From left: Sonny Tuft, Stork, Director W.S. Van Dyke and de Havilland.*

Bibliography

Doolittle, J. H. *I Could Never Be So Lucky Again, An Autobiography of General James H. Doolittle with Carroll V. Glines,* Bantam Books, New York, 1991.

Emmens, Robert G. *Guests of the Kremlin,* The MacMillan Co., New York, 1949.

Glines, Carroll V. *Doolittle's Tokyo Raiders,* Van Nostrand Reinhold Co., New York, 1964 & 1981.

_____. *Four Came Home, The Gripping Story of the Survivors of Jimmy Doolittle's Two Lost Crews,* Pictorial Histories Publishing Co. Inc., Missoula, MT, 1995.

_____. *Master of the Calculated Risk, A Pictorial Biography of James H. "Jimmy" Doolittle,* Pictorial Histories Publishing Co. Inc., Missoula, MT, 2002.

Lawson, Ted W. *30 Seconds Over Tokyo,* Random House, New York, 1943.

Nelson, Craig. *The First Heroes, The Extraordinary Story of the Doolittle Raid—America's First World War II Victory,* Viking, New York, 2002.

Reynolds, Quentin. *The Amazing Mr. Doolittle,* Appleton-Century-Crafts, Inc., New York, 1953.

Watson, C. Hoyt. *The Amazing Story of Sergeant Jacob DeShazer,* Light and Life Press, Winona Lake, Indiana, 1950.

The author holding a replica of the "Mark Twain" bombsight used on the Tokyo Raid.

About the Author

STAN B. COHEN is a native of West Virginia and has a degree in geology from West Virginia University. After many years working as a geologist, ski shop operator and director of an historical park, he established Pictorial Histories Publishing Company in Missoula, Montana, in 1976.

Since then he has authored or coauthored 80 books and published over 300. Some of his aviation titles include: *The Alaska Flying Expedition; Flying Beats Work: A Pictorial History of Reeve Aleutian Airways; Hawaiian Airlines, a Pictorial History; Wings to the Orient* and *The First Flight Around the World, April 6–Sept. 28, 1924.*

He lives in Missoula with his wife, Anne, and travels the world researching books and attending military reunions.